The Yale Edition of the Works of St. Thomas More
SELECTED WORKS

Published by the St. Thomas More Project,
Yale University, under the auspices of
Gerard L. Carroll and Joseph B. Murray,
Trustees of the Michael P. Grace, II, Trust

Woodcut map of Utopia from the March 1518 edition

ST. THOMAS MORE
☙UTOPIA☙

Edited with
Introduction and Notes by

EDWARD SURTZ, S. J.

NEW HAVEN AND LONDON, YALE UNIVERSITY PRESS

Library of the Congress catalog card number: 61–14944
International standard book numbers: 0–300–00980–1 (clothbound)
0–300–00238–6 (paperbound)

Designed by Crimilda Pontes and set in Baskerville Roman types. Printed in the United States of America by BookCrafters, Inc., Fredericksburg, Virginia.

The paper in this book meets the guidelines for permanence and durability of the Committee on Production Guidelines for Book Longevity of the Council on Library Resources.

36   35   34   33   32   31   30   29   28   27

CONTENTS

INTRODUCTION

UTOPIA PAST AND PRESENT

Utopia at first sight appears to be a book mad from great learning, but it turns out to be sober truth. What is its mysterious appeal that it should be put into practice by a Spanish judge and bishop among Indians in Mexico and yet should belong to the canonical books of the Communists—that it should be approved by Christian scholars of the Renaissance and by socialistic thinkers of the past two centuries—that it should be revered as a sacred volume by theists, deists, and atheists?

Can the essential reason be its humanism? Profoundly understood and deeply felt in the heart, its humanism undercuts particular political, philosophical, and religious systems and concerns itself with man as man. The *Utopia* thus achieves great universality by evincing great understanding and sympathy with all men. Like tragedy, even though it needs "a local habitation and a name," it deals with the ultimates of good and evil, virtue and vice, "justice and continence and the judgment that is to come." Even the social problems which appear in it are common and perennially recurrent: poverty and wealth, labor and property, education and health, food and clothing and housing. More importantly, the whole is suffused with two of the tenderest of all human feelings: pity and hope. The pity for the undeserved misery of the exploited poor is underscored by the indignation leveled at gentlemen, nobles, and abbots who lift not a finger to remove unbearable burdens. The hope for far better things, sustained by the view (so typically Renaissance) that man may shape and mold himself in any chosen form, is embodied in an apocalyptic vision of the best earthly state possible—Utopia.

Hence the curious ambivalence of detachment and involvement on our part. The perfect state, expressing in its details and in the ensemble a nonexistent ideal, is a work of art which detaches us from actuality and from self in sheer contemplation of beauty and goodness. Insofar as our own experiences, however, are reflected in the new creation, the *Utopia* implicates our feelings and consciences and gently forces our renewed commitment to justice, equity, and charity.

If we see our own experience given definitive expression in the *Utopia*, we may also find in the book a reflection of its author's being. In fact, close analysis of the text reveals that Thomas More has put a surprising amount of himself—his character, his biography, and his era—into his work, however much he might transcend his life and world by the timelessness of his art and vision.

Although the principal narrator, Thomas More, ingeniously presents himself as a minor character, quite subordinate to the engrossing Raphael Hythlodaeus, the latter's account attains a remarkable degree of immediacy and circumstantiality precisely because it comes to us colored by More's mentality and style. Early but indirectly he sketches his own portrait with a light and rapid brush: his importance (as a royal commissioner), his recognition of ability (as in the Provost of Cassel), his appreciation of friendship (as in the case of Tunstal and Giles), his love of family (in his pain at the four months' absence from England), his spirit of religion (incidentally revealed in his exit from Notre Dame after mass), his courtesy and hospitality (particularly toward Hythlodaeus), his love of a garden (used as a setting for the whole discourse), his intellectual curiosity (about foreign travel and especially about wise institutions), and his loyalty (toward his earliest patron, Cardinal Morton). His apology for prudent accommodation in kings' councils, his summary of anticommunistic arguments, and his disapproval of Utopian religion, warfare, and communism are open to varied interpretation. Not so his muted eagerness, expressed at the very end, for the European adoption of many Utopian institutions.

The *Utopia* appears to be so much the prophetic vision of a very young man that one is almost surprised to learn that More began to write his masterpiece at the age of thirty-seven. He has packed an amazing amount of autobiographical material into his work. London as his birthplace and residence is reflected in the capital city of Amaurotum, his years at Oxford in the pre-sunrise lectures in Utopia, and his lodging with the Carthusians in the verdict on the stricter Utopian ascetics as less wise but more holy. His studies and lectures at the Inns of Court are reflected in Hythlodaeus' controversy with the lawyer, his judicial duties as under-sheriff in the Utopian judge's acceptance of the most obvious argumentation and interpretation, his membership in parliament in the procedures for the Utopian senate, his service as royal commissioner in the two kings' councils, and his involvement with the London merchants in the opening lines and in the war between the Nephelogetes and the Alaopolitans. Even his more personal relationships as wooer, husband, and father may find expression in Utopian views on premarital offenses and adultery, marriage and divorce, the education of children, and the management of the household. (There is silence only on his role as widower and on his remarriage.)

Since More's rare talent for making and holding friends finds voice in the first edition of *Utopia* (as witnessed by his praise of Morton, Tunstal, and Giles, not to mention Busleyden's prefatory letter), one can only marvel at his silence on Erasmus. *Sed dum tacet, clamat.* Though silent, the *Utopia* cries aloud on this point: it pays Erasmus the sincerest flattery—that of imitation. Readers "knew not which soul spake, / Because both meant, both spake the same." This sameness in thinking and feeling rises to the surface in the use of proverbs and other materials from Erasmus' *Adages;* in the satirization of persons such as hunters, gamblers, lawyers, courtiers, philosophers, theologians, and popes, pilloried also in Erasmus' *Praise of Folly* (1511); and in the sound advice to kings, given summarily in the royal councils in *Utopia* but developed lengthily in Erasmus' *Education of a Christian Prince* (1516).

In addition to self-characterization and autobiography, More has astonishingly numerous references, direct or indirect, to the historical background. As for the national scene, explicit mention is made of the Cornish insurrection, suppressed at Blackheath (June 1497), and of the controversial enclosures of the common land, the first great wave of which was now nearing its end. The second royal council in Book I points obliquely to the growing Tudor absolutism, particularly in the creation of the Star Chamber and in the new financial system, efficient though arbitrary, ruthlessly executed by Morton, Dudley, and Empson. Sometimes a few words contain a topical allusion. In the opening paragraph, the epithet *invincible* could refer to the victories at Guinegate and Flodden Field (1513), and "certain weighty matters" indubitably relates to problems arising from the recent commercial treaties with the Low Countries, the *Intercursus Magnus* (1496) and the *Intercursus Malus* (1506).

The international situation, finding its focus in the first royal council in Book I, is instinctively epitomized in the ambitions of the French kings—from Charles VIII, whose invasion in 1494 turned Italy into the battleground of Europe for decades, to Francis I, whose victory at Marignano in September 1515 made him the envy of princes. The mercenary character of the Swiss whom he defeated is satirized in the Zapoletans. There are countless "submerged" allusions. The very choice of the setting, Antwerp, foreshadows the city's rapid growth into the commercial and financial center of Europe in the sixteenth century. The Portuguese nationality of Hythlodaeus symbolizes the zenith of Portuguese power and empire under Manuel I (and John III) after the great discoveries of Gama and Cabral. (There is, of course, explicit mention of the pilot major of Spain, Amerigo Vespucci.) The flagrant violation of treaties and alliances comes in for deserved condemnation. Even the diplomatic double-dealing of the popes, particularly Julius II, is pilloried ironically. The emphasis upon education and learning, especially upon Greek, manifests the accelerating conquest of northern Europe by the Italian Renaissance. Finally, the crowning chapter on religion underlines the serious ecclesiastical and spiritual problems on the eve of the Reformation.

Thus the *Utopia* at least touches on the movements which are said to characterize essentially the height of the Renaissance (approx. 1492–1520): the consolidation of absolute monarchy in kingdoms and principalities; the establishment of dynasticism as the controlling factor in international affairs; the decline in the power and prestige of the Catholic clergy, as indicated by the attack on the pope, monks, and friars and by the positive picture of ascetics who work hard and of bishops and priests who restrict themselves—and are restricted—to spiritual affairs; and the triumph of humanism—in the religious sphere, as in the simple piety of the Utopians, and in the secular realm, as in its anti-Scholasticism and its stress on the Greek classics. It is therefore no accident that the

Utopia

Utopia, being part and parcel of its epoch, was composed and published in a decade that saw the composition or publication of *The Prince, The Courtier, Orlando Furioso, The Praise of Folly*, and Erasmus' edition of the New Testament. The *Utopia* belongs with these golden books of the Golden Age of the Renaissance.

It is extremely difficult to assess the indebtedness of the *Utopia* to humanistic documents of the Renaissance for the simple reason that More, like almost all other humanists, does not acknowledge the use or the influence of contemporary works. In his edition of *The Education of a Christian Prince*, for example, L. K. Born lists more than thirty similarities with the *Utopia*. Erasmus' treatise is the best of the many Renaissance manuals which displace the medieval "mirror for princes" (*speculum principum*) and which may have influenced More in various ways. Francesco Patrizi's *Republic* (1471–84) is perhaps the only important treatise before the *Utopia* which intentionally treats the state as a whole. Political theory usually takes the form of advice to the prince and often is centered upon certain key virtues. Sometimes counsel is given indirectly—by way of recommendations for the education of princes, as in the case of Enea Silvio Piccolomini (Pius II) and Francesco Filelfo, not to mention again Erasmus.

No matter to what humanists he may be indebted, More uses certain classical sources in common with them. He shows familiarity with such standard treatises on statecraft as those by Isocrates, Xenophon, Aristotle, and Dio Chrysostom; but the most evident influences are Plato, in both the *Republic* and the *Laws,* and Plutarch, particularly in the life of Lycurgus of Sparta. Nor should one overlook the content and style of the *Germania* of Tacitus. For ethical and philosophical doctrines, particularly Stoicism and Epicureanism, the main sources are Diogenes Laertius, Cicero, and Seneca. The tone of the *Utopia* may owe something to Lucian's "wit and pleasantry." Contrary to likely conjecture, Augustine's *City of God,* on which More had lectured publicly, seems to have influenced *Utopia* only in a quite general and vague way. The same could be said for the best medieval political treatises, such as those by John of Salisbury or Thomas Aquinas.

All in all, *Utopia* contains hardly a detail for which the scholar cannot find a source or an analogue in classical, patristic, medieval, or humanistic works. Some of the pleasure to be experienced in reading *Utopia* arises precisely from the recognition of familiar and common features. Yet the novelty of More's masterpiece is universally acknowledged. The small fragments of colored stone and glass are pieced together to form a picture of incomparable design. In a word, the originality of the *Utopia* lies less in the details than in the ensemble or the whole.

Utilizing contemporary excitement over geographical exploration and discovery, Thomas More has Hythlodaeus light upon the ideal state—actually existent and not in the process of formation as are Plato's commonwealths. In delineating this state, More does not employ mere essay or dialogue but gives fictional and dramatic form to what elsewhere is expounded theoretically or advocated categorically. To give an obvious example, flattery is not condemned in the abstract but in action— in the vivid scene before Cardinal Morton. In regard to substance and organization, one discovers that while other humanists had centered their discussions upon an educational program, or upon the citizen, or upon the prince, More has dealt with a whole nation. Apparently Patrizi alone had undertaken such a feat before him and then in a conventional and encyclopedic manner.

Nowhere, perhaps, is the originality of *Utopia* more pronounced than in two most important and controversial features: its hedonism and its communism. One need make no bones about the clear fact that pleasure is the end and goal of the Utopian state. If Utopia is the best form of commonwealth, it must necessarily look to the well-being of all its citizens, and for the latter the height of well-being is pleasure. In this renewed emphasis on the joys of mortal life and the delights of earth, the Utopians are typical Renaissance men, who juggle the philosophies of apparently classical Epicureanism and of so-called medieval Christianity until, a happy reconciliation and balance being achieved, they can have the best of both worlds. The individual Utopians pursue personal pleasure until it conflicts with social or religious duties, that is, with the just claims of God or fellow citizens. The term *pleasure* (*voluptas*), therefore, is necessarily used in a very wide and loose sense: it embraces everything pleasant, from the scratching of an itch to a self-approving conscience and eternal beatitude. In practice, because the performance of good and virtuous deeds is the source of the greatest pleasure, More stoicizes Epicureanism just as Erasmus, by making Christ the Epicurean *par excellence*, Christianizes it.

Appreciation of the basic Utopian philosophy, that of pleasure, helps to bring Utopian communism into proper perspective. It is not an end in itself but the best means to the end: pleasure for all the citizens collectively as well as individually. Here the classical sources are at once reinforced and modified by the reputed communism of Christ and His disciples in the gospels and of the primitive Church in the Acts. Whereas only Plato's rulers, potential and actual, appear to practice communism, the whole nation of Utopians is communistic. Instead of extending communism to wives and children as Plato did, *Utopia* emphasizes the unity of the family—although in a youthful *declamatio* More had included wives in his defense of Plato's communism. A popular militia replaces

Introduction

Plato's professional soldiery, a representative democracy his aristocracy. A practical philosophy of pleasure supplants a highly theoretical philosophy centered on the contemplation of the good and the beautiful. Instead of Socrates' prudent refusal to tamper with religion, a lengthy concluding chapter in *Utopia* is devoted to faith and worship—to say nothing of previous references to God and Christ. Not philosophy but religion is at the core of Utopian existence, and even if the latter statement be minimized, it cannot be denied that religion is woven inextricably into the fabric of the *Utopia*. What appears in the work is not the mere common possession of material goods like food, clothing, and shelter, but also the active communion of all things intellectual and spiritual: a free striving after a common education, culture, philosophy, and religion. The ultimate Utopian ideal of communism is this: to be of one mind, to think the same thoughts, so that they "may all have but one heart and one mouth." Sharing material possessions can succeed only if there is first but one heart and soul in all.

This view would have been grasped immediately by all contemporary humanists—and More was writing particularly for men like Erasmus, Giles, and Tunstal—who could read between the lines and could understand the implications of a phrase, a character, or an incident. It is evident from their letters and works that they shared at this time a common outlook on their world. Being accustomed to adapt classical ideals to Christian principles, they realized that it was a strange and harmless hedonism which at the top of its hierarchy of pleasures placed intellectual pursuits, consciousness of a virtuous soul, and union with God in heaven. They realized that behind Utopian communism lay the espousal of Christian communion, the common sharing of all things: good and bad, prosperous and adverse, joyful and sorrowful, including even wealth and poverty, health and sickness, life and death. The popularity of works like the *Praise of Folly* and the *Letters of Obscure Men* shortly before had accustomed them to oblique technique and indirect interpretation: they knew that what More was actually doing was expressing their common ideas. Such was the frame of mind of the first, and for More the most important, readers of *Utopia*.

Undoubtedly the feeling that they had a common lot in the *Utopia* explains the interest of the contributors to the earliest editions in having More's work succeed. Although he excluded himself from the first edition, Erasmus, as More's friend and mentor, was naturally the party most zealous for an auspicious launching. Prominent humanists like Busleyden, Giles, Geldenhauer, and Schrijver gave him eager cooperation, which was climaxed by the renowned Budé's letter for the second edition.[1] All entered wholeheartedly into the fiction of the existence of Hythlodaeus and the Utopians. The work must have succeeded beyond all their expectations. Sent by More to Erasmus under date of September 3, 1516, it was first published by Thierry Martens at Louvain, most probably in December. The second edition, edited by Thomas Lupset for the Parisian press of Gilles de Gourmont, appeared the next year. The famous publisher, John Froben of Basel, issued two editions, in March and November 1518, with a prefatory letter by Erasmus. These were followed by the Florentine Giunti's undistinguished edition in 1519. The last edition in which More had a direct hand appears to be that of March 1518. The latter, therefore, can be viewed as the best, or at least the basic, text.

1. For these letters see Vol. 4 of The Yale Edition of the Complete Works of St. Thomas More. The present volume includes only the first letter (1516) from More to Peter Giles. It also omits the marginal glosses (probably written by Giles and Erasmus) which appeared in the early editions.

Introduction

Friendly humanists would be interested not only in More's ideas, but also and especially in his literary techniques. More has of course selected as his linguistic medium the Latin language, which, far from seeming antique and artificial, was living, mature, and up-to-date. Besides, Latin was the only language in which More could communicate across international borders with his fellow humanists—and with all cultured and learned men. The second device, the adoption of which would appear quite natural to them, was that of dialogue, a genre consecrated from its use by their beloved Plato—to say nothing of Cicero, Augustine, Petrarch, and others. They would note, however, a difference. Whereas Plato's dialogue is dialectic, that is, the continuing, reasoning inquiry of philosophers after a truth, More's is narrative, the account of a conversation in a garden with a world-traveler who includes a lengthy description of an ideal state in his report.

A third technique calling for humanistic admiration would be More's wise choice of a central point of view. The state of Utopia is almost too good to be true: consequently its description by means of an observant visitor is an aid to credibility. The picture is given quite objectively. For the most part, More lets Hythlodaeus' words speak for themselves and does not inject his personal interpretation; the major exception occurs at the very end of the *Utopia*. It goes without saying that More feels strongly on important matters, but he advances his cause by muting his own sensibilities and by allowing Hythlodaeus free and full expression. The frequent complexity of the form, dialogue within dialogue in a narrative frame, reflects the complexity of the problems—but More achieves simplification by focusing on the account of Hythlodaeus.

This is a fourth aspect that the humanists would find laudable. Unity is attained through keeping Hythlodaeus at the center of the stage. On the question of the best state he meets all challengers—and triumphs in his way, at least by leaving the field undefeated. Hence the strong sense of conflict shared with the readers. Hythlodaeus doughtily battles the lawyer on capital punishment and on enclosure, the royal councilors on foreign and domestic policies, Thomas More himself on the traditional arguments against communism, and Peter Giles in his defense of European superiority. All these points, of course, are side issues of the main conflict: the nature of the best state. The picture of actually existent Utopia (which, like Arthur's diamond shield, suddenly and accidentally uncovered against Orgoglio, "Such blazing brightnesse through the ayer threw / That eye mote not the same endure to vew") subdues and silences all opposition. What line of argumentation can prevail against a hard fact like Utopia? The result of silencing all opposition, of course, is that the victor in Book II now engages in a prolonged monologue—or perhaps it is more just and fair to call Hythlodaeus' description of Utopia a one-sided dialogue. Like a dramatic monologue in Browning, it contains answers and arguments against the implied queries or objections of his auditors. Nevertheless the account is less lively and exciting, warm and personal, than the active dialogue and direct quotation of Book I.

The tendency to monotony in Hythlodaeus' travelogue, humanists would observe, is offset by two other expedients. The first is frequent contrast with conditions in Europe. This contrast may be explicit, as in the comparison between the handful excused from manual labor in Utopia and the hordes of idle women, clergy, wealthy noblemen, retainers, and beggars in Europe; or it may be implicit, as in the case of the reverent silence in Utopian temples compared with the noisy atmosphere in European churches. The second means, resorted to in

Introduction

Book II oftener than in Book I, is the use of comedy. Erasmus in 1511, Pace in 1517, and Rhenanus in 1518 all lay stress on More's jesting. In this respect, humanists in 1516 most probably found the *Utopia* to be much more a *libellus festivus,* "an entertaining, merry handbook," than we. "What is to prevent one from telling truth as he laughs?" as Horace had said. The range of the comic element is great: irony, as in the reference to the popes (such as Alexander VI and Julius II) who conscientiously keep their own promises and religiously require that those called the "faithful" should "faithfully adhere to their alliances"; satire, as in the ridicule of foolish pleasures like hunting and gambling; humor, as in the dazzling entrance and subsequent humiliation of the Anemolian ambassadors; farce, as in the conversion of gold bullion into chamber pots or chains for slaves; and outright laughter at the incongruous, as at the custom of pre-marital inspection of prospective bride and groom. A remarkable feature of the frequent comic tone is not only that it helps to furnish relief. In almost every case it also emphasizes the thought and reinforces the emotional context.

An analysis of the emotional element in Book I reveals that the dominant pity for the poor and indignation over injustice are varied by a philosopher's love of liberty, by contempt and repugnance toward the sycophantic courtiers, by resentment at the suggestions of the timeserving royal councilors, and by an attitude of intransigence toward halfway measures. The admiration, love, and hope which underlie the objective description of Utopia in Book II, however, are less diversified than the feelings in Book I. They are varied mainly, as we have seen, by comic touches. But the description is followed by a perfervid peroration which runs the gamut of all the passions previously excited in both books. Humanists of yesterday and today would become intensely involved.

The emotions have solid intellectual foundations and maintain a careful balance and proportion with the subject matter: hence they never sound either flat and dull or loud and shrill.

The temptation would be to the latter, in fact, almost to hysterical passion, because of the gravity of the evils being exposed and denounced. Much of the success in the control of the emotional element is connected with More's effective characterization of Hythlodaeus. The latter is a philosopher, not a demagogue. It is his rational emotions that determine those of the humanist readers. Neither in his own person nor through the eyes of friend or enemy does More give any lengthy or elaborate description. Instead he builds up Hythlodaeus' character stroke by stroke. He discloses each trait as it is called forth and needed by successive situations. The character of this major figure, in a way, is still emerging and developing at the end. Since the *Utopia* is not a drama in the strict sense, he cannot reveal himself through his actions (except as narrated); instead, the principal method of characterization is through what he says of himself and how he says it.

Our introduction to Hythlodaeus is skillful and gradual: first, his physical appearance through More's eyes; secondly, his traveler's background through Giles' thumbnail sketch given to More; and, lastly, his views and attitudes in his own words. As a philosopher, his attachment to freedom is such that he must reject royal service. The courtiers, councilors, and kings with whom he would have to associate are enemies to what he holds dearest: reason and truth, freedom and open-mindedness, justice and peace. All his sympathies are therefore with the poor, the oppressed, the workers, the propertyless. Because of his philosophic principles as well as his experiences in Utopia and elsewhere, he indignantly rejects the course of accommodation proposed by More, impatiently re-

Introduction

futes halfway measures, and takes an uncompromising
stand for the elimination of money and property. The
necessity of this policy is clear to him from Utopia. He
announces and testifies to what he has heard, what he has
seen with his eyes, what he has looked upon and his
hands have handled: "you should have been with me in
Utopia and personally seen their manners and customs
as I did." After his detailed description, he rises to the
stature of a prophet, who thunders against injustice and
greed and pride and who climaxes his harangue with a
joyful apocalyptic vision of holy Utopia. Almost as if
blinded and weakened by the revelation, he is meekly
taken by the hand and led indoors by More at the close
of the work.

Hythlodaeus' function is clear. He succeeds in making
his readers share his sentiments: pity, scorn, indignation,
hope, love, and admiration. If his world be black and
white, if his men be saints or devils, if his communistic
republic is too perfect and his propertied state too vil-
lainous, this idealist and his personality are offset by the
other characters: John Morton, impatient, unprejudiced,
experienced, and progressive; Peter Giles, simple in pro-
posing a royal councilorship, loyal in his defense of
European superiority, and curious about Utopia; and
Thomas More himself, friendly, tactful, and inquisitive
—to say nothing of the argumentative lawyer, the foolish
toady, and the inept friar. But, alas, what should one
make of the faceless Utopians in their perfect state? Even
Utopus appears, not individualized as a person, but
masked as an able king on a garden island.

At any rate, the focus upon Hythlodaeus helps to pin-
point the theme: it can be none other than "The Best
State of a Commonwealth"—to use modern equivalents:
the best form of government or, preferably, the best order of society. Unlike the individual headings of the two
books, only the title on the front page includes the

words: "and the New Island of Utopia." And rightly so. The description of Utopia is actually but part of the whole. Only convenience has given the work the short appellation *Utopia* rather than the more correct but clumsy title: *The Best State of a Commonwealth.* The main practical problem for the interlocutors is the achievement of justice for the poor laboring classes and therefore for the whole nation. A *good* state could be attained by various provisional and palliative measures (which are listed at intervals by Hythlodaeus himself, e.g. in the two royal councils), but the *best* state, insists Hythlodaeus, can result only from a radical change and innovation: the adoption of communism.

At first sight the development of this theme seems haphazard and disorderly. Actually the work, being centered on Hythlodaeus, is simplicity itself. After a brief exposition of setting, characters, tone, and theme, the great debate on councilorship ensues. The debate falls into three sections corresponding to the three reasons urged upon Hythlodaeus for being a royal councilor: (1) its advantage for his family and himself (answered by reflections on sycophantic courtiers as dramatized in the discussion before Cardinal Morton on capital punishment for robbery: its causes, necessity, utility, and replacement); (2) the philosopher's duty to advise rulers (refuted by the picture of the two royal councils, the one on foreign affairs, the other on domestic policies); and (3) the obligation not to desert the storm-tossed ship of state but to use the principle of accommodation (rejected by references to Christ's doctrine, Plato's communism, and Utopia's existence). A brief pause for midday dinner ends Book I. It is well to remember that the debate on councilorship fits into the whole precisely as one possible means to the attainment of the best commonwealth. But, like all means short of communism, it is rejected by Hythlodaeus.

Introduction

Book II can be divided into four great sections: (1) the overall view of Utopia—geographical, political, economic, and social—given succinctly and forcefully; (2) the philosophical and educational foundations, treated in detail because important; (3) household matters (miscellaneous), war, and religion; and (4) the passionate summation of his position by Hythlodaeus. A few concluding words by Thomas More constitute the denouement.

In his last remarks More singles out the three major problems created for him (as representative of Christians and Europeans) by Utopian mores: the conduct of war, rites and religion, and the system of communism (not to mention such relatively minor problems as slavery, divorce, and euthanasia). Hedonism and communism have been touched on already. As for the Utopian "habit of bidding for and purchasing an enemy" and other dastardly military tactics, these are reflections of actual contemporary practices. If Europeans condemn the Utopians, they condemn none other than themselves, who also rationalize and justify evil means to an apparently good end. As for their great common religion, it shadows forth many reforms needed in the Church: clerical sanctity, reverence in church, simple music, joyful resignation to death, etc. All is ready for triumphant fulfillment in Christ and Christianity. Contemporary humanists would have grasped this fact immediately.

Humanists would also have appreciated the Latin style of *Utopia*. More is far from being a narrow Ciceronian; instead, he shows the flexibility and breadth demonstrated by Erasmus in *De duplici copia verborum ac rerum* (1512). In fact, just as More was composing the *Utopia*, Erasmus praised the improvement in style of his Latin letters. In his controversy with More, Germanus Brixius, in spite of his boast, could find few solecisms and barbarisms in the *Utopia*. More's vocabulary, except for a hundred words or so, is classical. His sentences are loose rather than periodic, and they favor parallelism. Congruent with the adoption of the dialogue form, the level of expression is usually colloquial rather than formal. Therefore the main merits of the style are force and clarity rather than elegance and purity. Because G. C. Richards has captured many qualities of the Latin original, his English translation[2] forms the basis of the present version: easy, cultured, and conversational but geared to the emotional nuances and exigencies, particularly the tension and relaxation, of Hythlodaeus' discourse.

Figurative language is perhaps less difficult to convey in a translation than are syntax and diction. More's most startling metaphor is the one most frequently quoted from *Utopia* over the centuries: that of the erstwhile harmless sheep who now "devour human beings themselves and devastate and depopulate fields, houses, and towns." In general, however, More uses quite commonplace figures; he instinctively keeps them brief lest elaboration disclose their inherent triteness and obviousness. Contrary to expectation, he rarely employs the fertile notion of the ship of state. Much more in keeping with his diagnosis of an ailing and diseased society, he avails himself of medical metaphors, particularly healing and remedy. He applies them also to individuals sick from vice, folly, or madness. Not infrequent are agricultural metaphors, especially in regard to sowing or to uprooting the ills of the commonwealth. Animal comparisons are abundant: workers being like beasts of burden, hardened convicts like untamed beasts, and mercenary soldiers like wild beasts. The idle rich are like drones, the humbled vainglorious like crestfallen fowl, a prospective

2. First published, Oxford, 1923. The text printed here, which incorporates a number of revisions by the editor, is issued with the permission of Sir Basil Blackwell. For Latin text see Vol. 4 of The Yale Edition of the Complete Works.

wife like a colt to be purchased, antiquated laws like moth-eaten clothes, and pride like a goddess, a serpent, and a suckfish. Such human institutions as the stage and prison form the basis for comparisons, as do human occupations like those of seafarer, schoolmaster, priest, muleteer, and shepherd.

Symbolism is not neglected. If there be a symbol for the whole first book, it is the gallows for thieves: "as many as twenty at a time being hanged on one gallows." For More the gallows must be representative of systematic social injustice: the disproportionate punishment of hanging for thievery, which thievery is occasioned by expulsion from farms and homes on account of enclosures, which enclosures are caused by the profits from sheep-grazing, which profits arouse the greed of the idle rich, which idle rich thrive on the exploitation of the poor, which exploitation can flourish only because of private property and pride—which private property and pride can and must be eliminated by communism. There is frantic grasping for money and power on all sides—by the rich always squeezing a few more pennies from the poor, by the rulers ever seeking to add more revenues to their treasury or more provinces or kingdoms to their realm. And if the entire second book has a symbol, it is that of the common dining hall which abounds in good things and pleasures. Each meal taken together stands for the triumph of justice and equity and represents the equality and communion of all the citizens.

Is there possibly a symbol for the *Utopia* as a whole? If one exists, it is, in a broad sense, that of the dialogue. All *Utopia* is a dialogue on the ideal commonwealth. Within it is the dialogue on royal councilorship as an effective means to the best state. Within this dialogue on counsel are, first, the dialogue on capital punishment before Cardinal Morton and, secondly, the dialogues on foreign and domestic affairs in the two privy councils conjured up by Hythlodaeus' imagination. On the island of Utopia there appears to be constant dialogue, the most important topics being furnished by philosophy and religion. Finally, the great common prayer reads as a dialogue with God.

Is the success of *Utopia* due to dialogue? After all, dialogue is symbolic of open-mindedness, humility, and inquiry. Somehow or other, More succeeds in involving readers in the dialogue. It is no accident that the *Utopia* ends with challenges. Is the Utopian view of war, religion, and communism really absurd? Is the Utopian vision really hopeless and unachievable? The *Utopia* therefore is an open-ended work—or, better, a dialogue with an indeterminate close. More asks the right questions—which can never be answered fully. He poses the right problems—which can never be solved completely. The fight for justice and equity—with pen and sword— is never ended as long as vice and folly, greed and ignorance, pride and prejudice, influence or possess human minds and hearts.

Precisely because the *Utopia* is a dialogue between characters which provokes dialogue between readers, interpretations show wide variation, even sharp contradiction. Michelet, Knox, Campbell, and others have tended to stress the literary aspects with the consequent emergence of the *Utopia* as primarily a *jeu d'esprit* of a Renaissance humanist. This position is rendered weak by the length and gravity of the description of Utopia and by the numerous references, express or covert, to English abuses and European malpractices, as well as by the verdicts of More's contemporaries. On the more serious side, Kautsky, Oncken, Ames, and others have found in *Utopia* the active espousal, even though disguised, of measures like communism, colonialism, imperialism, and democracy. Stress on political, social, and economic innovations, however, tends to make More appear too farsighted and to sever him from his environment or to give a lopsided view of his *Utopia*: just as important are the opinions, fully developed, on education, learning, ethics, philosophy, and religion. In fact, except for some neglect of the fine arts (only music and architecture being referred to), Hythlodaeus paints a relatively complete picture of all aspects of the state. Utopia is a pagan state, newly discovered, but it need be changed very little to become a Christian state. For Thomas More as a Christian humanist, grace builds upon nature, revelation complements reason, Christianity fulfills preexisting religions.

R. W. Chambers declares: "The underlying thought of *Utopia* always is, *With nothing save Reason to guide them, the Utopians do this; and yet we Christian Englishmen, we Christian Europeans . . . !*" This interpretation is perhaps too narrow and too moralistic: too narrow because God and religion, Christ and revelation, play a clear part in the *Utopia,* especially at critical junctures, and too moralistic because the primary purpose of the *Utopia* is not the exhortation of sinning Christians but the delineation of the ideal commonwealth.

Hythlodaeus is the only utopian idealist in More's book. He holds the presuppositions of utopianism: man's natural goodness and irreducible rationality, the desirability and attainability of a secure and happy society on this earth, the feasibility of planning and the ability of individuals to adapt themselves to a planned society, the possibility of fatherly rulers and of the free obedience of subjects, the avoidance of a clash between the individual who wants a free life and the society which asks his free cooperation, and, finally, faith in the permanence of the ideal state without fatigue or tedium on the part of its inhabitants. The anti-utopians (or "dystopians," to use J. Max Patrick's excellent term) faced by Hythlodaeus are the princes, who busy themselves with war and conquest and who, impervious to advice, need first to be philosophers themselves; the courtiers and councilors, who are self-conceited in their wisdom, sycophantic, faultfinding, and tenacious of traditional practices (the poorer ones); the lawyer, interested only in argument and fearful of "bringing the state into the gravest crisis"; and, in his fictional role, Thomas More himself, urging the principle of accommodation and maintaining: "it is impossible that all should be well unless all men were good—a situation which I do not expect for a great many years to come!" In communism, More argues, the individual is "rendered slothful by trusting to the industry of others." Even Peter Giles will not admit Utopian superiority to Europe in brains or experience—although Hythlodaeus finds that Europeans, totally unlike Utopians, will not adopt any better institutions and practices. The very last words in More's book say that there are many Utopian features "which it is easier for me to wish for in our states than to have any hope of seeing realized." More thus gives himself the role of doubting Thomas—the first dystopian man of letters!

But Thomas More portrays himself mainly as an embryonic dystopian. The full-fledged dystopian sees man as an everlasting and inseparable blend of good and evil, as a creature of impulses and prejudices as well as mind and reason. In this view, man is material so plastic that he can be made by conditioning and brainwashing to think himself a free cooperator in his society, whereas he is actually its slave, a member of a society planned as good but likely to be unforeseeably perverted into a cruel absurdity. Thus man as ruler is corrupted inevitably by power, and, as citizen, even in the happiest utopia, he becomes bored, restless, desirous of change for change's sake. Significantly, More has forestalled these objections. Utopians are not saints: all need to be educated carefully, and some do become criminals—in spite of the

severe punishment meted out to them. A degree of lee-
way for differences in individuality and personality is
permitted in the choice of a manual occupation, the use
of leisure, and the expression of heterodoxy. Rulers "are
called fathers and show that character. Honor is paid
them willingly." Most important of all, Utopia does not
represent a system, closed and fixed, permanent and perfect. In spite of Hythlodaeus' last words on its eternity,
it is like the literary work in which it is enshrined: it is
open-ended, at least in theory and intention.

In the great common prayer, which significantly uses
the singular number, each Utopian asks God to let him
know whether there is a state better and happier and
more pleasing to Him: he is ready to accept and adopt
it. Each Utopian is thereby admonished to keep an open
mind—which prevents a closed system. This is the first
safeguard against dystopia. The second is a philosophy
and a religion which make man's final end to be, not
worship of the state, but union with the Absolute.
Through their government the Utopians "offer honors to
invite men to virtue"; but it is also God who, for personal sacrifices made for public benefits, "repays in place
of a brief and tiny pleasure immense and never-ending
gladness." Hence Utopians need to believe in the soul's
immortality and in future rewards. In the great common
prayer, the individual prefers "to die a very hard death
and go to God than to be kept longer away from Him
even by a very prosperous career in life."

Utopian absolutes are Christian values thinly veiled.
There is a provident God who watches good and evil,
who rewards virtue or vice, who is concerned about man's
government. In Utopia it is the citizens most motivated
by religion who show the greatest charity and helpful-
ness toward their fellow citizens. Utopia recognizes and
solves the problem of equality and inequality, of differences in degree: the rulers show themselves loving fa-

thers, the subjects show themselves lovingly obedient. The value of the individual personality is acknowledged because it transcends the Utopian state through motivation by divine love in this life and through a union with God in the next. In a word, the happiness of the next world becomes the inspiration for creating happiness in this world.

Has More seized here on the clue to the discomfiture of the dystopian and to the realization of utopianism: the need for some transcendent philosophy and religion? It would seem so. In his novel *Island* (1962), the author of *Brave New World* presents a society of men who attempt to see science and technology not as a master but as an instrument and to cooperate rationally and calmly, as he had postulated earlier, in "the conscious and intelligent pursuit of man's Final End, the unitive knowledge of the immanent Tao or Logos, the transcendent Godhead or Brahman." And in the most practical application of More's *Utopia* to date, the hospital-villages of Santa Fe established by Don Vasco de Quiroga near Mexico City and in Michoacán, the whole atmosphere is redolent of apostolic and primitive Christianity. In a word, the function of the anti-utopia has been to make clear that political, social, and economic factors by themselves are insufficient to create a utopia. Building better than he knew, perhaps building instinctively from an innately good nature, More includes and utilizes forces that are cultural and intellectual, religious and spiritual. For him as the product of early sixteenth-century Western Europe, the forces are Christian and humanistic. Today's utopian visionary can choose from the great philosophies and religions of the world and time.

EDWARD SURTZ, S.J.

Loyola University of Chicago
June 1964

BIBLIOGRAPHY

I. GENERAL BIBLIOGRAPHY

For a selective bibliography of More's life and times, the reader is referred to *St. Thomas More: Selected Letters,* ed. E. F. Rogers (New Haven, 1961), pp. xix–xxiii. Among recent books are the following:

ADAMS, ROBERT P., *The Better Part of Valor,* Seattle, 1962.

HOGREFE, PEARL, *The Sir Thomas More Circle,* Urbana, 1959.

MARC'HADOUR, GERMAIN, *L'Univers de Thomas More,* Paris, 1963.

SYLVESTER, R. S., and D. P. HARDING, eds., *Two Early Tudor Lives: . . . Wolsey, by George Cavendish . . . More, by William Roper,* New Haven, 1962.

II. *UTOPIA* AND UTOPIAN LITERATURE

St. Thomas More: A Preliminary Bibliography, eds. R. W. Gibson and J. Max Patrick (New Haven, 1961), contains an invaluable section, "Utopias and Dystopias, 1500–1750," pp. 291–412. On pp. 301–05 there is "A Short-Title List of Some Bibliographies and Books about Utopias and Related Literature." The following should be added to the list:

HERBRÜGGEN, HUBERTUS SCHULTE, *Utopie und Anti-Utopie,* Bochum-Langendreer, 1960.

WALSH, CHAD, *From Utopia to Nightmare,* New York, 1962.

Longer recent studies of More's *Utopia* itself are the following:

AMES, RUSSELL, *Citizen Thomas More and His Utopia*, Princeton, 1949.

DONNER, H. W., *Introduction to Utopia*, London, 1945.

HEXTER, J. H., *More's Utopia: The Biography of an Idea*, Princeton, 1952.

SURTZ, EDWARD, *The Praise of Pleasure*, Cambridge, Mass., 1957.

————, *The Praise of Wisdom*, Chicago, 1957.

III. SHORT TITLES IN FOOTNOTES

The best commentary on *Utopia* consists in cross references within the text itself. The footnotes to this edition have been kept to a minimum, frequently by omitting full references. The latter can be found in the bibliography and notes to Volume 4 (*Utopia*) of The Yale Edition of the Complete Works of St. Thomas More (New Haven, 1965), where far more attention is paid to the literature of the Renaissance. For Latin and Greek classics, the standard abbreviations (as used, for example, in *The Oxford Classical Dictionary*, Oxford, 1949) have been adopted. The texts and translations given in the notes are usually those of the Loeb Classical Library, published by the Harvard University Press.

AEG. ROM. *Reg. Prin.* Aegidius Romanus, *De regimine principum*, Venice, 1498.

BACON, *Henry VII.* Francis Bacon, *The Historie of the Reigne of King Henry the Seventh*, London, 1641.

ELYOT, *Gou.* Thomas Elyot, *The Boke Named the Gouernour*, ed. H. H. S. Croft, 2 vols. London, 1883.

Ep. obscur. vir. Epistolae obscurorum virorum, Latin Text with an English Rendering . . . by F. G. Stokes, London, 1925.

Bibliography

ERAS. *Adag.* Desiderius Erasmus, "Adagia," *Opera* (see below), Vol. II.

ERAS. *Ep.* *Opus epistolarum Des. Erasmi Roterodami,* ed. P. S. Allen et al., 12 vols. Oxford, 1906–58.

ERASMUS, *Colloquies.* *The Whole Familiar Colloquies,* tr. N. Bailey, London, 1877.

ERASMUS, *Folly.* *The Praise of Folly,* tr. H. H. Hudson, Princeton, 1941.

ERASMUS, *Opera.* *Opera omnia . . . studio et opera Joannis Clerici,* 10 vols. Leyden, 1703–06.

ERASMUS, *Prince.* *The Education of a Christian Prince,* tr. L. K. Born, New York, 1936.

FORTESCUE, *Gov.* John Fortescue, *The Governance of England,* ed. C. Plummer, Oxford, 1885.

HARPSFIELD. Nicholas Harpsfield, *The Life and Death of Sʳ Thomas Moore,* ed. E. V. Hitchcock, London, 1932 (reissued 1963).

HOLINSHED, *Chronicles.* Raphael Holinshed, *The Chronicles of England, Scotland, and Ireland,* 3 vols. in 2, London, 1587.

LUPTON, *Utopia.* J. H. Lupton, ed., *The Utopia of Sir Thomas More,* Oxford, 1895.

MACHIAVELLI, *Discourses.* Niccolò Machiavelli, *Discourses,* tr. L. J. Walker, 2 vols. London, 1950.

MACHIAVELLI, *Prince.* *The Prince and Other Works,* tr. A. H. Gilbert, Chicago, 1941.

MORE, *Comp. Works.* The Yale Edition of the Complete Works of St. Thomas More, New Haven and London, vol. 2, 1963; vol. 4, 1965.

MORE, *Corresp.* *The Correspondence of Sir Thomas More,* ed. E. F. Rogers, Princeton, 1947.

MORE, *Epigr.* *The Latin Epigrams of Thomas More,* ed. and tr. L. Bradner and C. A. Lynch, Chicago, 1953.

MORE, *Opera.* *Omnia . . . Latina opera,* Louvain, 1565.

MORE, *S.L.* *St. Thomas More: Selected Letters,* ed. E. F. Rogers, New Haven, 1961.

MORE, *Utopia.* *De optimo reip. statu deque noua insula Vtopia libellus . . . Thomae Mori . . . ,* Basel, March 1518.

MORE, *Works.* *The workes of Sir Thomas More, . . . wrytten by him in the Englysh tonge,* London, 1557.

PATRIZI, *Reg.* Francesco Patrizi, *De regno et regis institutione,* Paris, 1567.

PATRIZI, *Rep.* Francesco Patrizi, *De institutione reipublicae,* Paris, 1534.

Relation of England. *A Relation, or Rather a True Account, of the Island of England . . . About the Year 1500,* tr. C. A. Sneyd, London, 1847.

ROPER. William Roper, *The Lyfe of Sir Thomas Moore,* ed. E. V. Hitchcock, London, 1935.

STAPLETON. Thomas Stapleton, *The Life and Illustrious Martyrdom of Sir Thomas More,* tr. P. E. Hallett, London, 1928.

STARKEY, *Dialogue.* Thomas Starkey, *A Dialogue Between Cardinal Pole and Thomas Lupset,* ed. J. M. Cowper, London, 1871.

VERGIL, *Ang. hist.* *The Anglica Historia of Polydore Vergil, A.D. 1485–1537,* tr. D. Hay, London, 1950.

VERGIL, *Eng. Hist.* *Polydore Vergil's English History, from an Early Translation . . . ,* Vol. I, ed. H. Ellis, London, 1846.

VERGIL, *Rer. invent.* *De rerum inventoribus libri octo,* Lyons, 1546.

VESPUCCI, *Quat. nav.* *Quatuor Americi Vespucij nauigationes,* St. Dié, 1507, in facsimile, in *The Cosmographiae Introductio of Martin Waldseemüller, Followed by the Four Voyages of Amerigo Vespucci, with Their Translations into English,* ed. C. G. Herbermann, New York, 1907. (Trans. of *Four Voyages* by M. E. Cosenza.)

ADDITIONAL BIBLIOGRAPHY

Since the original publication of this volume in 1964, a large number of studies of *Utopia* have been published. The following brief bibliography is only a sampling, but consultation of the items listed will quickly indicate the continuing appeal of More's master work.

Avineri, Shlomo, "War and Slavery in More's *Utopia*," *International Review of Social History*, 7 (1962), 260–90

Barker, Arthur E., "Clavis Moreana: The Yale Edition of Thomas More," *Journal of English and Germanic Philology*, 65 (1966), 318–330

Bleich, David, "More's *Utopia*: Confessional Modes," *American Imago* (1971), 24–52

Elliott, Robert C., *The Shape of Utopia: Studies in a Literary Genre*, Chicago, 1970

Johnson, Robbin S., *More's Utopia: Ideal and Illusion*, New Haven, 1969

Manuel, F. E., ed., *Utopias and Utopian Thought*, Boston, 1967. A valuable collection of essays.

Moreana, Nos. 31–32 (1971). The entire issue is devoted to *Utopia*.

Prévost, André, *Thomas More et la crise de la pensée européene*, Lille, 1969

Schoeck, R. J., " 'A Nursery of Correct and Useful Institutions': On Reading More's *Utopia* as Dialogue," *Moreana*, 22 (1969), 19–32

Seeber, Hans Ulrich, *Wandlungen der Form in der literarischen Utopia: Studien zur Entfaltung des utopischen Romans in England*, Göppingen, 1970

Sylvester, R. S., " 'Si Hythlodaeo Credimus': Vision and Revision in Thomas More's *Utopia*," *Soundings* (formerly *The Christian Scholar*), 51 (1968), 272–89

Since 1964 three additional volumes have been published in the Yale Edition of The Complete Works of St. Thomas More: vol. 3, pt. I, *Translations of Lucian*, 1974; vol. 5, *Responsio ad Lutherum*, 1969; vol. 8, *The Confutation of Tyndale's Answer*, 1973. Three volumes (vol. 12, *A Dialogue of Comfort*; vol. 13, *Treatise on the Passion*; vol. 14, *De Tristitia Christi*) are in press and scheduled for publication in 1976. The third volume in the Selected Works of St. Thomas More series, *King Richard III*, is also in press and scheduled for publication in the fall of 1975.

THE BEST
STATE OF A COMMONWEALTH
AND THE NEW ISLAND
OF UTOPIA

A Truly Golden Handbook,
No Less Beneficial than Entertaining,
by the Distinguished and Eloquent Author
THOMAS MORE
Citizen and Sheriff of the Famous City
of London

THOMAS MORE TO PETER GILES,
GREETINGS.

I am almost ashamed, my dear Peter Giles, to send you this little book about the state of Utopia after almost a year,[1] when I am sure you looked for it within a month and a half. Certainly you know that I was relieved of all the labor of gathering materials for the work and that I had to give no thought at all to their arrangement. I had only to repeat what in your company I heard Raphael relate. Hence there was no reason for me to take trouble about the style of the narrative, seeing that his language could not be polished. It was, first of all, hurried and impromptu[2] and, secondly, the product of a person who, as you know, was not so well acquainted with Latin as with Greek. Therefore the nearer my style came to his careless simplicity the closer it would be to the truth, for which alone I am bound to care under the circumstances and actually do care.

I confess, my dear Peter, that all these preparations relieved me of so much trouble that scarcely anything remained for me to do. Otherwise the gathering or the arrangement of the materials could have required a good

1. More's visit to Giles in Antwerp occurred probably in mid or late September 1515, after an absence of more than four months from London. It was almost a year later, on September 3, 1516, that he sent the *Utopia* to Erasmus (*S.L.*, p. 73).

2. Lat. *extemporalis*. More in London added the first book *ex tempore* (Eras. *Ep.*, *4*, 21) to the second book, already written in the Low Countries during the enforced leisure of his embassy.

deal of both time and application even from a talent neither the meanest nor the most ignorant. If it had been required that the matter be written down not only accurately but eloquently, I could not have performed the task with any amount of time or application. But, as it was, those cares over which I should have had to perspire so hard had been removed. Since it remained for me only to write out simply what I had heard, there was no difficulty about it.

Yet even to carry through this trifling task, my other tasks left me practically no leisure at all. I am constantly engaged in legal business, either pleading or hearing, either giving an award as arbiter or deciding a case as judge. I pay a visit of courtesy to one man and go on business to another. I devote almost the whole day in public to other men's affairs and the remainder to my own. I leave to myself, that is to learning, nothing at all.

When I have returned home, I must talk with my wife, chat with my children, and confer with my servants. All this activity I count as business when it must be done —and it must be unless you want to be a stranger in your own home. Besides, one must take care to be as agreeable as possible to those whom nature has supplied, or chance has made, or you yourself have chosen, to be the companions of your life, provided you do not spoil them by kindness, or through indulgence make masters out of your servants.

Amid these occupations that I have named, the day, the month, the year slip away. When, then, can we find time to write? Nor have I spoken a word about sleep, nor even of food, which for many people takes up as much time as sleep—and sleep takes up almost half a man's life! So I get for myself only the time I filch from sleep and food.[3] Slowly, therefore, because this time is

3. More composed the first book *per occasionem* (Eras. *Ep., 4,* 21), during minutes snatched from eating and sleeping.

but little, yet finally, because this time *is* something, I have finished *Utopia* and sent it to you, my dear Peter, to read—and to remind me of anything that has escaped me.

In this respect I do not entirely distrust myself. (I only wish I were as good in intelligence and learning as I am not altogether deficient in memory!) Nevertheless, I am not so confident as to believe that I have forgotten nothing. As you know, John Clement,[4] my pupil-servant, was also present at the conversation. Indeed I do not allow him to absent himself from any talk which can be somewhat profitable, for from this young plant, seeing that it has begun to put forth green shoots in Greek and Latin literature, I expect no mean harvest some day. He has caused me to feel very doubtful on one point.

According to my own recollection, Hythlodaeus declared that the bridge which spans the river Anydrus at Amaurotum is five hundred paces in length. But my John says that two hundred must be taken off, for the river there is not more than three hundred paces in breadth. Please recall the matter to mind. If you agree with him, I shall adopt the same view and think myself mistaken. If you do not remember, I shall put down, as I have actually done, what I myself seem to remember. Just as I shall take great pains to have nothing incorrect in the book, so, if there is doubt about anything, I shall rather tell an objective falsehood than an intentional lie[5]—for I would rather be honest than wise.

4. More uses almost the identical words in an earlier letter to Erasmus (*S.L.*, p. 72). Clement (d. 1572) became tutor to More's children, a Wolsey Reader at Oxford (1518), co-editor of the first Greek edition of Galen (1525), physician to Henry VIII (1528), and president of the College of Physicians (1544).

5. Lat. orig.: *potius mendacium dicam, quam mentiar, quod malim bonus esse quam prudens.* "One who lies (*mentitur*) is not himself deceived, but tries to deceive another; he who tells a falsehood (*mendacium*) is himself deceived. . . . A good man (*bonus*) . . . ought to take pains not to lie, a wise man (*prudens*), not to tell what is false" (Gell. *NA* 11.11.1–4).

Nevertheless, it would be easy for you to remedy this defect if you ask Raphael himself by word of mouth or by letter. You must do so on account of another doubt which has cropped up, whether more through my fault or through yours or Raphael's I do not know. We forgot to ask, and he forgot to say, in what part of the new world Utopia lies. I am sorry that point was omitted, and I would be willing to pay a considerable sum to purchase that information, partly because I am rather ashamed to be ignorant in what sea lies the island of which I am saying so much, partly because there are several among us, and one in particular, a devout man and a theologian by profession, burning with an extraordinary desire to visit Utopia. He does so not from an idle and curious lust for sight-seeing in new places but for the purpose of fostering and promoting our religion, begun there so felicitously.

To carry out his plan properly, he has made up his mind to arrange to be sent by the pope and, what is more, to be named bishop for the Utopians. He is in no way deterred by any scruple that he must sue for this prelacy, for he considers it a holy suit which proceeds not from any consideration of honor or gain but from motives of piety.

Therefore I beg you, my dear Peter, either by word of mouth if you conveniently can or by letter if he has gone, to reach Hythlodaeus and to make sure that my work includes nothing false and omits nothing true. I am inclined to think that it would be better to show him the book itself. No one else is so well able to correct any mistake, nor can he do this favor at all unless he reads through what I have written. In addition, in this way you will find out whether he accepts with pleasure or suffers with annoyance the fact that I have composed this work. If he himself has decided to put down in writing his own adventures, perhaps he may not want me to do so. By making known the commonwealth of Utopia, I should certainly dislike to forestall him and to rob his narrative of the flower and charm of novelty.

Nevertheless, to tell the truth, I myself have not yet made up my mind whether I shall publish it at all. So varied are the tastes of mortals, so peevish the characters of some, so ungrateful their dispositions, so wrongheaded their judgments, that those persons who pleasantly and blithely indulge their inclinations seem to be very much better off than those who torment themselves with anxiety in order to publish something that may bring profit or pleasure to others, who nevertheless receive it with disdain or ingratitude.

Very many men are ignorant of learning; many despise it. The barbarian rejects as harsh whatever is not positively barbarian. The smatterers despise as trite whatever is not packed with obsolete expressions. Some persons approve only of what is old; very many admire only their own work. This fellow is so grim that he will not hear of a joke; that fellow is so insipid that he cannot endure wit. Some are so dull-minded that they fear all satire[6] as much as a man bitten by a mad dog fears water. Others are so fickle that sitting they praise one thing and standing another thing.

These persons sit in taverns, and over their cups criticize the talents of authors. With much pontificating, just as they please, they condemn each author by his writings, plucking each one, as it were, by the hair. They themselves remain under cover and, as the proverb goes, out of shot. They are so smooth and shaven that they present not even a hair of an honest man by which they might be caught.[7]

6. Lat. *nasus,* 'nose,' the organ conceived to be expressive of anger, contempt, etc. Persons without a satiric sense are *simi,* 'flat-nosed,' here translated 'dull-minded.'

7. A figure taken from wrestling and popular with spiritual writers, e.g. Gregory the Great, *Hom.* 32.

Besides, others are so ungrateful that, though extremely delighted with the work, they do not love the author any the more. They are not unlike discourteous guests who, after they have been freely entertained at a rich banquet, finally go home well filled without thanking the host who invited them. Go now[8] and provide a feast at your own expense for men of such dainty palate, of such varied taste, and of such unforgetful and grateful natures!

At any rate, my dear Peter, conduct with Hythlodaeus the business which I mentioned. Afterwards I shall be fully free to take fresh counsel on the subject. However, since I have gone through the labor of writing, it is too late for me to be wise now. Therefore, provided it be done with the consent of Hythlodaeus, in the matter of publishing which remains I shall follow my friends' advice, and yours first and foremost. Good-by, my sweetest friend, with your excellent wife.[9] Love me as you have ever done, for I love you even more than I have ever done.

8. Cf. Chaucer, *Troilus* 5.1786, and Eras. *Adag.* 2001.

9. For the wedding with Cornelia in 1514, Erasmus promised the colloquy *Epithalamium Petri Aegidii*, published ten years later.

THE BEST STATE OF A COMMONWEALTH,[1]
THE DISCOURSE OF THE EXTRAORDINARY CHARACTER, RAPHAEL HYTHLODAEUS, AS REPORTED BY THE RENOWNED FIGURE, THOMAS MORE, CITIZEN AND SHERIFF[2] OF THE FAMOUS CITY OF GREAT BRITAIN, LONDON

BOOK I

The most invincible[3] King of England, Henry, the eighth of that name, who is distinguished by all the accomplishments of a model monarch, had certain weighty matters[4] recently in dispute with His Serene Highness, Charles, Prince of Castile.[5] With a view to their discussion and settlement, he sent me as a commissioner to Flanders—as

1. Modern equivalents: "the nature of an ideal constitution," "the best form of government," or "the best order of society."

2. More became under-sheriff on September 3, 1510. This officer was important as supervisor of prisoners, executioner of writs, legal adviser, and judge (cf. Eras. *Ep.*, *4, 20*).

3. An honorific title, merited in 1513 by Henry's personal triumph in the Battle of the Spurs and in the occupation of Tournai and Thérouanne and by his subjects' victory at Flodden.

4. The possible seizure of the entire English merchant fleet for back payment of various tolls.

5. In 1515 the future Charles V (1500–58) was not yet king. His grandfather, Ferdinand of Aragon, was regent for his mother, Juana the Mad, until his death in January 1516.

a companion and associate of the peerless Cuthbert Tunstal,[6] whom he has just created Master of the Rolls[7] to everyone's immense satisfaction. Of the latter's praises I shall say nothing, not because I fear that the testimony of a friend should be given little credit but because his integrity and learning are too great for it to be possible, and too well-known for it to be necessary, for me to extol them—unless I should wish to give the impression, as the proverb goes, of displaying the sun with a lamp![8]

We were met at Bruges, according to previous arrangement, by those men put in charge of the affair by the Prince—all outstanding persons.[9] Their leader and head was the Burgomaster of Bruges,[10] a figure of magnificence, but their chief speaker and guiding spirit was Georges de Themsecke,[11] Provost of Cassel,[12] a man not only trained in eloquence but a natural orator—most learned, too, in the law and consummately skillful in diplomacy by native ability as well as by long experience. When after one or two meetings there were certain points on which we could not agree sufficiently, they bade farewell to us for some days and left for Brussels[13]

6. Tunstal (1474–1559), More's lifelong and close friend, named in More's epitaph, Bishop of London (1522) and Durham (1530). Other distinguished commissioners were R. Sampson, Bishop of Chichester (1536) and of Coventry and Lichfield (1543); W. Knight, Bishop of Bath and Wells (1541); T. Spinelly, professional diplomat; and J. Clifford, Governor of the English Merchants. The commissions were dated May 7 and October 2, 1515.

7. On May 12, 1516. At this time this official was the chief assistant to the Lord Chancellor.

8. Cf. Eras. *Adag.* 658, 1406, 1407, 3725.

9. For their conjectural identification see *Cath. Hist. Rev., 39* (1953), 272–97.

10. J. de Halewyn, Seigneur de Maldeghem.

11. Employed on numerous important diplomatic missions, he died in 1536.

12. Now in the Département du Nord, France.

13. Charles was at Brussels from July 23 to 29, 1515.

Book I

to seek an official pronouncement from the Prince.

Meanwhile, as my business led me, I made my way to Antwerp.[14] While I stayed there, among my other visitors, but of all of them the most welcome, was Peter Giles,[15] a native of Antwerp, an honorable man of high position in his home town yet worthy of the very highest position, being a young man distinguished equally by learning and character; for he is most virtuous and most cultured, to all most courteous, but to his friends so open-hearted, affectionate, loyal, and sincere that you can hardly find one or two anywhere to compare with him as the perfect friend on every score. His modesty is uncommon; no one is less given to deceit, and none has a wiser simplicity of nature. Besides, in conversation he is so polished and so witty without offense that his delightful society and charming discourse largely took away my nostalgia and made me less conscious than before of the separation from my home, wife, and children to whom I was exceedingly anxious to get back, for I had then been more than four months away.[16]

One day I had been at divine service in Notre Dame,[17] the finest church in the city and the most crowded with worshippers. Mass being over, I was about to return to my lodging when I happened to see him in conversation with a stranger, a man of advanced years, with sunburnt countenance and long beard and cloak hanging carelessly from his shoulder, while his appearance and dress seemed to me to be those of a ship's captain.

14. Antwerp was "now one of the flowers of the world," according to More's colleague, Sampson (*LP*, 2, 160).

15. Giles (c. 1486–1533) is paid the same compliment in More's letter to Erasmus, February 1516 (*S.L.*, p. 71). Chief *griffier* (i.e. clerk of the court of justice) at Antwerp, he was also editor of Politian, Agricola, Aesop, Lucian, etc.

16. More had left London on May 12, 1515.

17. Incomplete in 1515, it became the cathedral when Antwerp was designated an independent diocese in 1559.

When Peter had espied me, he came up and greeted me. As I tried to return his salutation, he drew me a little aside and, pointing to the man I had seen him talking with, said:

"Do you see this fellow? I was on the point of taking him straight to you."

"He would have been very welcome," said I, "for your sake."

"No," said he, "for his own, if you knew him. There is no mortal alive today who can give you such an account of unknown peoples and lands, a subject about which I know you are always most greedy to hear."

"Well, then," said I, "my guess was not a bad one. The moment I saw him, I was sure he was a ship's captain."

"But you are quite mistaken," said he, "for his sailing has not been like that of Palinurus but that of Ulysses or, rather, of Plato.[18] Now this Raphael—for such is his personal name, with Hythlodaeus[19] as his family name— is no bad Latin scholar, and most learned in Greek.[20] He had studied that language more than Latin because he had devoted himself unreservedly to philosophy, and in that subject he found that there is nothing valuable in Latin except certain treatises of Seneca and Cicero.[21] He left his patrimony at home—he is a Portuguese—to his brothers, and, being eager to see the world, joined Amerigo Vespucci and was his constant companion in the last three of those four voyages which are now uni-

18. On Palinurus, see *Aen.* 5.833–61; on Ulysses, *Od.* passim; and on Plato, *Ep.* 7.323D–52A, and Diog. Laert. 3.6–7, 18–22.

19. Hythlodaeus: 'expert in trifles' or 'well-learned in nonsense.' Raphael: 'healing of God,' possibly chosen because of his role as guide to Tobias in his travels.

20. See More's 1518 Letter to Oxford University (*S.L.*, pp. 94– 103).

21. "If you leave out Cicero and Seneca, the Romans wrote their philosophy in Greek or translated it from Greek" (*S.L.*, p. 100).

versally read of,[22] but on the final voyage he did not
return with him. He importuned and even wrested from
Amerigo permission to be one of the twenty-four who at
the farthest point[23] of the last voyage were left behind
in the fort. And so he was left behind that he might have
his way, being more anxious for travel than about the
grave. These two sayings are constantly on his lips: 'He
who has no grave is covered by the sky,' [24] and 'From all
places it is the same distance to heaven.' [25] This attitude
of his, but for the favor of God, would have cost him
dear. However, when after Vespucci's departure he had
traveled through many countries with five companions
from the fort, by strange chance he was carried to Ceylon,
whence he reached Calicut.[26] There he conveniently
found some Portuguese ships, and at length arrived home
again, beyond all expectation."

When Peter had rendered this account, I thanked him
for his kindness in taking such pains that I might have a
talk with one whose conversation he hoped would give
me pleasure; then I turned to Raphael. After we had
greeted each other and exchanged the civilities which
commonly pass at the first meeting of strangers, we went
off to my house. There in the garden, on a bench covered
with turfs of grass,[27] we sat down to talk together.

22. The most famous account is *COSMOGRAPHIAE INTRO-
DVCTIO . . . Insuper quatuor Americi Vespucij nauigationes . . .*
(St. Dié in the Vosges, April 25, 1507).

23. Cape Frio in southeast Brazil.

24. Luc. 7.818–19; cf. Aug. *De Civ. D.* 1.12.

25. Attributed to Anaxagoras of Clazomenae in Cic. *Tusc.* 1.43.
104. More made a similar remark in the Tower (Roper, p. 83;
Harpsfield, p. 96).

26. Known to the ancients as Taprobane, Ceylon was discovered
by the Portuguese in 1505. Calicut was reached by Pero da Covil-
ham in 1486–87, visited by Vasco da Gama in 1498, replaced by
Goa as Portuguese headquarters in 1510.

27. Apparently a boxlike affair, filled with earth and topped with
sod. Cf. Chaucer: "a bench of turves, fresshe and grene" (*Merch
T* 2235).

He recounted how, after the departure of Vespucci, he and his friends who had stayed behind in the fort began by degrees through continued meetings and civilities to ingratiate themselves with the natives till they not only stood in no danger from them but were actually on friendly terms and, moreover, were in good repute and favor with a ruler (whose name and country I have forgotten). Through the latter's generosity, he and his five companions were supplied with ample provision and travel resources and, moreover, with a trusty guide on their journey (which was partly by water on rafts and partly over land by wagon) to take them to other rulers with careful recommendations to their favor. For, after traveling many days, he said, they found towns and cities and very populous commonwealths with excellent institutions.

To be sure, under the equator and on both sides of the line nearly as far as the sun's orbit extends, there lie waste deserts scorched with continual heat. A gloomy and dismal region looms in all directions without cultivation or attractiveness, inhabited by wild beasts and snakes or, indeed, men no less savage and harmful than are the beasts. But when you have gone a little farther, the country gradually assumes a milder aspect, the climate is less fierce, the ground is covered with a pleasant green herbage, and the nature of living creatures becomes less wild. At length you reach peoples, cities, and towns which maintain a continual traffic by sea and land not only with each other and their neighbors but also with far-off countries.

Then they had opportunity of visiting many countries in all directions, for every ship which was got ready for any voyage made him and his companions welcome as passengers. The ships they saw in the parts first traveled were flat-bottomed and moved under sails made of papyrus or osiers stitched together and sometimes under sails made of leather. Afterwards they found ships with pointed keels and canvas sails, in fact, like our own in all respects.

Their mariners were skilled in adapting themselves to sea and weather. But he reported that he won their extraordinary favor by showing them the use of the magnetic needle of which they had hitherto been quite ignorant so that they had hesitated to trust themselves to the sea and had boldly done so in the summer only. Now, trusting to the magnet, they do not fear wintry weather, being dangerously confident. Thus, there is a risk that what was thought likely to be a great benefit to them may, through their imprudence, cause them great mischief.

What he said he saw in each place would be a long tale to unfold and is not the purpose of this work. Perhaps on another occasion we shall tell his story, particularly whatever facts would be useful to readers, above all, those wise and prudent provisions which he noticed anywhere among nations living together in a civilized way. For on these subjects we eagerly inquired of him, and he no less readily discoursed; but about stale travelers' wonders we were not curious. Scyllas and greedy Celaenos and folk-devouring Laestrygones[28] and similar frightful monsters are common enough, but well and wisely trained citizens are not everywhere to be found.

To be sure, just as he called attention to many ill-advised customs among these new nations, so he rehearsed not a few points from which our own cities, nations, races, and kingdoms may take example for the correction of their errors. These instances, as I said, I must mention on another occasion. Now I intend to relate merely what he told us of the manners and customs of the

28. For Scylla and Celaeno, see Verg. *Aen.* 3.209–58, 424–32; for the Laestrygones, Hom. *Od.* 10.77–132.

Utopians, first, however, giving the talk which drew and led him on to mention that commonwealth.

Raphael had touched with much wisdom on faults in this hemisphere and that, of which he found very many in both, and had compared the wiser measures which had been taken among us as well as among them; for he remembered the manners and customs of each nation as if he had lived all his life in places which he had only visited. Peter expressed his surprise at the man as follows:

"Why, my dear Raphael, I wonder that you do not attach yourself to some king. I am sure there is none of them to whom you would not be very welcome because you are capable not only of entertaining a king with this learning and experience of men and places but also of furnishing him with examples and of assisting him with counsel. Thus, you would not only serve your own interests excellently but be of great assistance in the advancement of all your relatives and friends."

"As for my relatives and friends," he replied, "I am not greatly troubled about them, for I think I have fairly well performed my duty to them already. The possessions, which other men do not resign unless they are old and sick and even then resign unwillingly when incapable of retention, I divided among my relatives and friends when I was not merely hale and hearty but actually young. I think they ought to be satisfied with this generosity from me and not to require or expect additionally that I should, for their sakes, enter into servitude to kings."

"Fine words!" declared Peter. "I meant not that you should be in servitude but in service to kings."

"The one is only one syllable less than the other," [29] he observed.

29. *Servitude* (or *slavery*) has three syllables; *service*, two. *Inseruias* has one syllable more than *seruias* in the Latin original.

Book I

"But my conviction is," continued Peter, "whatever name you give to this mode of life, that it is the very way by which you can not only profit people both as private individuals and as members of the commonwealth but also render your own condition more prosperous."

"Should I," said Raphael, "make it more prosperous by a way which my soul abhors? As it is, I now live as I please,[30] which I surely fancy is very seldom the case with your grand courtiers. Nay, there are plenty of persons who court the friendship of the great, and so you need not think it a great loss if they have to do without me and one or two others like me."

"Well," I then said, "it is plain that you, my dear Raphael, are desirous neither of riches nor of power. Assuredly, I reverence and look up to a man of your mind no whit less than to any of those who are most high and mighty. But it seems to me you will do what is worthy of you and of this generous and truly philosophic spirit[31] of yours if you so order your life as to apply your talent and industry to the public interest, even if it involves some personal disadvantages to yourself. This you can never do with as great profit as if you are councilor to some great monarch and make him follow, as I am sure you will, straightforward and honorable courses. From the monarch, as from a never-failing spring, flows a stream of all that is good or evil over the whole nation. You possess such complete learning that, even had you no great experience of affairs, and such great experience of affairs that, even had you no learning, you would make an excellent member of any king's council."

30. Cicero's definition of liberty (*Off.* 1.20.70), often quoted in the Renaissance. On the philosopher's love of liberty, see More's translations (*Works*, pp. 8, 14).

31. See Plutarch, "That a Philosopher Ought to Converse Especially with Men in Power" (*Mor.* 776A–79C); Erasmus' Latin translation appeared in 1516.

"You are twice mistaken, my dear More," said he, "first in me and then in the matter in question. I have no such ability as you ascribe to me and, if I had ever so much, still, in disturbing my own peace and quiet, I should not promote the public interest. In the first place almost all monarchs[32] prefer to occupy themselves in the pursuits of war—with which I neither have nor desire any acquaintance—rather than in the honorable activities of peace, and they care much more how, by hook or by crook, they may win fresh kingdoms than how they may administer well what they have got.

"In the second place, among royal councilors everyone is actually so wise as to have no need of profiting by another's counsel, or everyone seems so wise in his own eyes as not to condescend to profit by it, save that they agree with the most absurd sayings of, and play the parasite to, the chief royal favorites whose friendliness they strive to win by flattery. To be sure, it is but human nature that each man favor his own discoveries most—just as the crow and the monkey like their own off-spring best.[33]

"If anyone, when in the company of people who are jealous of others' discoveries or prefer their own, should propose something which he either has read of as done in other times or has seen done in other places, the listeners behave as if their whole reputation for wisdom were jeopardized and as if afterwards they would deserve to be thought plain blockheads unless they could lay hold of something to find fault with in the discoveries of others. When all other attempts fail, their last resource is a remark such as this: 'Our forefathers were happy with that sort of thing, and would to heaven we had their wisdom.' And then, as if that comment were a bril-

32. See the French council below and Eras. *Adag.* 1401.
33. Cf. More's *Works*, p. 845, and Eras. *Adag.* 115, 121, 3964.

liant conclusion to the whole business, they take their seats—implying, of course, that it would be a dangerous thing to be found with more wisdom on any point than our forefathers. And yet, no matter what excellent ideas our forefathers may have had, we very serenely bid them a curt farewell. But if in any situation they failed to take the wiser course, that defect gives us a handle which we greedily grab and never let go. Such proud, ridiculous, and obstinate prejudices I have encountered often in other places and once in England too."

"What," I asked, "were you ever in our country?"

"Yes," he answered, "I spent several months there, not long after the disastrous end of the insurrection of western Englishmen[34] against the king, which was put down with their pitiful slaughter. During that time I was much indebted to the Right Reverend Father, John Cardinal Morton,[35] Archbishop of Canterbury, and then also Lord Chancellor of England. He was a man, my dear Peter (for More knows about him and needs no information from me), who deserved respect as much for his prudence and virtue as for his authority. He was of middle stature and showed no sign of his advanced age. His countenance inspired respect rather than fear. In conversation he was agreeable, though serious and dignified. Of those who made suit to him he enjoyed making trial by rough address, but in a harmless way, to see what mettle and what presence of mind a person would manifest. Provided it did not amount to impudence, such behavior gave him pleasure as being akin to his own disposition and excited his admiration as being suited to those holding public office. His speech was polished and pointed.

34. That is, Cornishmen, in 1497 (Vergil, *Ang. hist.*, tr. Hay, pp. 90–99).

35. This prelate and statesman (c. 1420–1500) receives similar praise in More's *Richard III* (*Comp. Works*, 2, 90–91).

His knowledge of law was profound, his ability incomparable, and his memory astonishingly retentive, for he had improved his extraordinary natural qualities by learning and practice.

"The king placed the greatest confidence in his advice, and the commonwealth seemed much to depend upon him when I was there. As one might expect, almost in earliest youth he had been taken straight from school to court, had spent his whole life in important public affairs, and had sustained numerous and varied vicissitudes of fortune, so that by many and great dangers he had acquired a statesman's sagacity which, when thus learned, is not easily forgotten.

"It happened one day that I was at his table when a layman, learned in the laws[36] of your country, was present. Availing himself of some opportunity or other, he began to speak punctiliously of the strict justice which was then dealt out to thieves. They were everywhere executed, he reported, as many as twenty at a time being hanged on one gallows, and added that he wondered all the more, though so few escaped execution, by what bad luck the whole country was still infested with them. I dared be free in expressing my opinions without reserve at the Cardinal's table, so I said to him:

" 'You need not wonder, for this manner of punishing thieves goes beyond justice and is not for the public good. It is too harsh a penalty for theft and yet is not a sufficient deterrent. Theft alone[37] is not a grave offense that ought to be punished with death, and no penalty that can be devised is sufficient to restrain from acts of robbery those who have no other means of getting a livelihood. In this respect not your country alone but a

36. The legal profession was often a means to wealth, fame, and power (cf. Eras. *Ep.*, *4*, *17*).

37. A simple theft, unattended by violence or murder.

Book I

great part of our world resembles bad schoolmasters, who would rather beat than teach their scholars.[38] You ordain grievous and terrible punishments for a thief when it would have been much better to provide some means of getting a living, that no one should be under this terrible necessity first of stealing and then of dying for it.'

" 'We have,' said the fellow, 'made sufficient provision for this situation. There are manual crafts. There is farming. They might maintain themselves by these pursuits if they did not voluntarily prefer to be rascals.'

" 'No,' I countered, 'you shall not escape so easily. We shall say nothing of those who often come home crippled from foreign or civil wars, as recently with you Englishmen from the battle with the Cornishmen and not long ago from the war in France.[39] They lose their limbs in the service of the commonwealth or of the king, and their disability prevents them from exercising their own crafts, and their age from learning a new one. Of these men, I say, we shall take no account because wars come sporadically, but let us consider what happens every day.

" 'Now there is the great number of noblemen who not only live idle themselves like drones[40] on the labors of others, as for instance the tenants of their estates whom they fleece to the utmost by increasing the returns (for that is the only economy they know of, being otherwise so extravagant as to bring themselves to beggary!) but who also carry about with them a huge crowd of idle attendants who have never learned a trade for a livelihood. As soon as their master dies or they them-

38. Like Plato (*Rep.* 7.536D–37A), Quintilian (*Inst.* 1.3.13–18), and Ps.-Plut. (*Mor.* 8F), Renaissance educators protested against compulsion and flogging.

39. At Dixmude (1489), Boulogne (1492), and, after this colloquy, in Guienne (1512) and at Thérouanne and Tournai (1513).

40. Cf. Pl. *Rep.* 8.552C–D.

selves fall sick, these men are turned out at once,[41] for the idle are maintained more readily than the sick, and often the heir is not able to support as large a household as his father did, at any rate at first.

" 'In the meantime the fellows devote all their energies to starving, if they do not to robbing. Indeed what can they do? When by a wandering life they have worn out their clothes a little, and their health to boot, sickly and ragged as they are, no gentleman deigns to engage them and the farmers dare not do so either. The latter know full well that a man who has been softly brought up in idleness and luxury and has been wont in sword and buckler to look down with a swaggering face on the whole neighborhood and to think himself far above everybody will hardly be fit to render honest service to a poor man with spade and hoe, for a scanty wage, and on frugal fare.'

" 'But this,' the fellow retorted, 'is just the sort of man we ought to encourage most. On them, being men of a loftier and nobler spirit than craftsmen and farmers, depend the strength and sinews of our army when we have to wage war.'

" 'Of course,' said I, 'you might as well say that for the sake of war we must foster thieves.[42] As long as you have these men, you will certainly never be without thieves. Nay, robbers do not make the least active soldiers, nor do soldiers make the most listless robbers, so well do these two pursuits agree.[43] But this defect, though frequent with you, is not peculiar to you, for it is common to almost all peoples.

" 'France in particular is troubled with another more grievous plague. Even in peacetime (if you can call it

41. For More's kindly treatment of his own servants, see *Works,* p. 1209, and Stapleton, p. 96.
42. Cf. Pl. *Rep.* 9.575B.
43. Cf. Aug. *De Civ. D.* 4.4.

peacetime) the whole country is crowded and beset with mercenaries hired because the French follow the train of thought you Englishmen take in judging it a good thing to keep idle retainers. These wiseacres[44] think that the public safety depends on having always in readiness a strong and reliable garrison, chiefly of veterans, for they have not the least confidence in tyros. This attitude obliges them always to be seeking for a pretext for war just so they may not have soldiers without experience, and men's throats must be cut without cause lest, to use Sallust's witty saying, "the hand or the mind through lack of practice become dulled." [45] Yet how dangerous it is to rear such wild beasts France has learned to its cost, and the examples of Rome, Carthage, Syria,[46] and many other nations[47] show. Not only the supreme authority of the latter countries but their land and even their cities have been more than once destroyed by their own standing armies.

" 'Now, how unnecessary it is to maintain them is clearly proved by this consideration: not even the French soldiers, assiduously trained in arms from infancy, can boast that they have very often got the better of it face to face with your draftees.[48] Let me say no more for fear of seeming to flatter you barefacedly. At any rate, your town-bred craftsmen or your rough and clodhopper farmers are not supposed to be much afraid of those idle

44. *Morosophi*, 'foolishly wise,' used in Lucian's *Alexander* and Erasmus' *Praise of Folly*.

45. Sall. *Cat.* 16.

46. On Rome and Carthage cf. Machiavelli's *Prince*, Chaps. 12–13; on Syria cf. Polyb. 5.31–87. In his "Dialogue of Comfort" (*Works*, p. 1219), More refers to the Ottoman conquest of Syria in 1516.

47. At this time, especially Italy and the Netherlands.

48. Undoubtedly a reference to Crécy (1346), Poitiers (1356), Agincourt (1415), and the Battle of the Spurs (1513). Machiavelli comments favorably on the English in his *Discourses*, 1.21.

attendants on gentlemen, except those of the former whose build of body is unfitted for strength and bravery or those whose stalwart spirit is broken by lack of support for their family. Consequently there is no danger that those attendants whose bodies, once strong and vigorous (for it is only the picked men that gentlemen deign to corrupt), are now either weakened by idleness or softened by almost womanish occupations, should become unmanned if trained to earn their living in honest trades and exercised in virile labors!

" 'However the case may be, it seems to me by no means profitable to the common weal to keep for the emergency of a war a vast multitude of such people as trouble and disturb the peace. You never have war unless you choose it, and you ought to take far more account of peace than of war. Yet this is not the only situation that makes thieving necessary. There is another which, as I believe, is more special to you Englishmen.'

" 'What is that?' asked the Cardinal.

" 'Your sheep,'[49] I answered, 'which are usually so tame and so cheaply fed, begin now, according to report, to be so greedy and wild that they devour human beings themselves and devastate and depopulate fields, houses, and towns. In all those parts of the realm[50] where the finest and therefore costliest wool is produced, there are noblemen, gentlemen, and even some abbots, though otherwise holy men, who are not satisfied with the annual revenues and profits which their predecessors used to derive from their estates. They are not content, by leading an idle and sumptuous life, to do no good to

49. On the whole problem see M. Beresford, *The Lost Villages of England* (London, 1954). The great number of sheep always struck foreign visitors and became proverbial on the continent.

50. The Inner Midlands (Northamptonshire, Oxfordshire, Warwickshire, Buckinghamshire, Leicestershire, Nottinghamshire) saw "intense depopulation c. 1450–1520" (Beresford, p. 220).

their country; they must also do it positive harm. They leave no ground to be tilled; they enclose every bit of land for pasture; they pull down houses and destroy towns, leaving only the church to pen the sheep in. And, as if enough of your land were not wasted on ranges and preserves of game, those good fellows turn all human habitations and all cultivated land into a wilderness.

" 'Consequently, in order that one insatiable glutton[51] and accursed plague of his native land may join field to field and surround many thousand acres with one fence, tenants are evicted. Some of them, either circumvented by fraud or overwhelmed by violence, are stripped even of their own property, or else, wearied by unjust acts, are driven to sell. By hook or by crook the poor wretches are compelled to leave their homes—men and women, husbands and wives, orphans and widows, parents with little children and a household not rich but numerous, since farm work requires many hands. Away they must go, I say, from the only homes familiar and known to them, and they find no shelter to go to. All their household goods which would not fetch a great price if they could wait for a purchaser, since they must be thrust out, they sell for a trifle.

" 'After they have soon spent that trifle in wandering from place to place, what remains for them but to steal and be hanged—justly, you may say!—or to wander and beg. And yet even in the latter case they are cast into prison as vagrants for going about idle when, though they most eagerly offer their labor, there is no one to hire them. For there is no farm work, to which they have been trained, to be had, when there is no land for plowing left. A single shepherd or herdsman is sufficient for grazing livestock on that land for whose cultivation many hands were once required to make it raise crops.

51. *helluo:* cf. Ter. *Haut.* 1033.

" 'A result of this situation is that the price of food has risen steeply in many localities. Indeed, the price of raw wools has climbed so high that your poor people who used to make cloth cannot possibly buy them, and so great numbers are driven from work into idleness. One reason is that, after the great increase in pasture land, a plague carried off a vast multitude of sheep as though God were punishing greed by sending upon the sheep a murrain—which should have fallen on the owners' heads more justly! But, however much the number of sheep increases, their price does not decrease a farthing because, though you cannot brand that a monopoly which is a sale by more than one person, yet their sale is certainly an oligopoly, for all sheep have come into the hands of a few men, and those already rich, who are not obligated to sell before they wish and who do not wish until they get the price they ask.

" 'By this time all other kinds of livestock are equally high-priced on the same account and still more so, for the reason that, with the pulling down of farmsteads and the lessening of farming, none are left to devote themselves to the breeding of stock. These rich men will not rear young cattle as they do lambs, but they buy them lean and cheap abroad and then, after they are fattened in their pastures, sell them again at a high price. In my estimation, the whole mischief of this system has not yet been felt. Thus far, the dealers raise the prices only where the cattle are sold, but when, for some time, they have been removing them from other localities faster than they can be bred there, then, as the supply gradually diminishes in the markets where they are purchased, great scarcity must needs be here.

" 'Thus, the unscrupulous greed of a few is ruining the very thing by virtue of which your island was once counted fortunate in the extreme. For the high price of food is causing everyone to get rid of as many of his household as possible, and what, I ask, have they to do but to beg, or—a course more readily embraced by men of mettle—to become robbers?

" 'In addition, alongside this wretched need and poverty you find wanton luxury. Not only the servants of noblemen but the craftsmen and almost the clodhoppers themselves, in fact all classes alike, are given to much ostentatious sumptuousness of dress[52] and to excessive indulgence at table. Do not dives, brothels, and those other places as bad as brothels, to wit, taverns, wine shops and ale-houses—do not all those crooked games of chance, dice, cards, backgammon, ball, bowling, and quoits, soon drain the purses of their votaries and send them off to rob someone?

" 'Cast out these ruinous plagues. Make laws[53] that the destroyers of farmsteads and country villages should either restore them or hand them over to people who will restore them and who are ready to build. Restrict this right of rich individuals to buy up everything and this license to exercise a kind of monopoly for themselves. Let fewer be brought up in idleness. Let farming be resumed and let cloth-working be restored once more that there may be honest jobs to employ usefully that idle throng, whether those whom hitherto pauperism has made thieves or those who, now being vagrants or lazy servants, in either case are likely to turn out thieves. Assuredly, unless you remedy these evils, it is useless for you to boast of the justice you execute in the punishment of theft. Such justice is more showy than really just or beneficial. When you allow your youths to be badly brought up and their characters, even from early years,

52. More has an epigram: "To Eupariphus, Who Mortgaged His Farm to Buy Clothing" (*Epigr.*, p. 211).

53. See Beresford, pp. 102–06, on the statutes against depopulation, and pp. 106–11, 116–22, 218–20, 317–23 on the commissions of inquiry.

to become more and more corrupt, to be punished, of course, when, as grown-up men, they commit the crimes which from boyhood they have shown every prospect of committing, what else, I ask, do you do but first create thieves and then become the very agents of their punishment?'

"Even while I was saying these things, the lawyer had been busily preparing himself to reply and had determined to adopt the usual method of disputants who are more careful to repeat what has been said than to answer it, so highly do they regard their memory.

" 'Certainly, sir,' he began, 'you have spoken well, considering that you are but a stranger who could hear something of these matters rather than get exact knowledge of them—a statement which I shall make plain in a few words. First, I shall repeat, in order, what you have said; then I shall show in what respects ignorance of our conditions has deceived you; finally I shall demolish and destroy all your arguments. So, to begin with what I promised first, on four points you seemed to me—'

" 'Hold your peace,' interrupted the Cardinal, 'for you hardly seem about to reply in a few words if you begin thus. So we shall relieve you of the trouble of making your answer now, but we shall reserve your right unimpaired till your next meeting, which I should like to set for tomorrow, provided neither you nor Raphael here is hindered by other business.

" 'But now I am eager to have you tell me, my dear Raphael, why you think that theft ought not to be punished with the extreme penalty, or what other penalty you yourself would fix, which would be more beneficial to the public. I am sure that not even you think it ought to go unpunished. Even as it is, with death as the penalty, men still rush into stealing. What force and what fear, if they once were sure of their lives, could deter the criminals? They would regard themselves as much invited to crime by the mitigation of the penalty as if a reward were offered.'

" 'Certainly,' I answered, 'most reverend and kind Father, I think it altogether unjust that a man should suffer the loss of his life for the loss of someone's money. In my opinion, not all the goods that fortune can bestow on us can be set in the scale against a man's life. If they say that this penalty is attached to the offense against justice and the breaking of the laws, hardly to the money stolen, one may well characterize this extreme justice as extreme wrong.[54] For we ought not to approve such stern Manlian[55] rules of law as would justify the immediate drawing of the sword when they are disobeyed in trifles nor such Stoical [56] ordinances as count all offenses equal so that there is no difference between killing a man and robbing him of a coin when, if equity has any meaning, there is no similarity or connection between the two cases.

" 'God has said, "Thou shalt not kill," and shall we so lightly kill a man for taking a bit of small change? But if the divine command against killing be held not to apply where human law justifies killing, what prevents men equally from arranging with one another how far rape, adultery, and perjury are admissible? God has withdrawn from man the right to take not only another's life but his own.[57] Now, men by mutual consent agree on definite cases where they may take the life of one

54. Cf. Cic. *Off.* 1.10.33 and the explanation in Eras. *Adag.* 925.

55. Manlius Torquatus, after forbidding single encounters with the enemy in the Latin War of 340 B.C., executed his own son for fighting and defeating a Latin champion (Livy 8.7.1–22).

56. The Stoic position is refuted in Cic. *Mur.* 29.61–30.63, *Fin.* 4.9.21–23, 4.27.75–77, and in Aug. *Ep.* 167 (*PL, 33,* 733–41).

57. But note the conditioned practice of euthanasia in Book II below.

another. But if this agreement among men is to have such force as to exempt their henchmen from the obligation of the commandment, although without any precedent set by God they take the life of those who have been ordered by human enactment to be put to death, will not the law of God then be valid only so far as the law of man permits? The result will be that in the same way men will determine in everything how far it suits them that God's commandments should be obeyed.

" 'Finally, the law of Moses,[58] though severe and harsh —being intended for slaves, and those a stubborn breed— nevertheless punished theft by fine and not by death. Let us not suppose that God, in the new law of mercy in which He gives commands as a father to his sons, has allowed us greater license to be cruel to one another.

" 'These are the reasons why I think this punishment unlawful. Besides, surely everyone knows how absurd and even dangerous to the commonwealth it is that a thief and a murderer should receive the same punishment. Since the robber sees that he is in as great danger if merely condemned for theft as if he were convicted of murder as well, this single consideration impels him to murder the man whom otherwise he would only have robbed. In addition to the fact that he is in no greater danger if caught, there is greater safety in putting the man out of the way and greater hope of covering up the crime if he leaves no one left to tell the tale. Thus, while we endeavor to terrify thieves with excessive cruelty, we urge them on to the destruction of honest citizens.

" 'As to the repeated question about a more advisable form of punishment, in my judgment it is much easier

58. On Jewish servitude as contrasted with Christian liberty cf. Gal. 2:4, 4:4–7, 4:24–31; Rom. 8:15; II Tim. 1:7. On Jewish stubbornness cf. Exod. 32:9, Deut. 9:13, Acts 7:51. On the new law of mercy cf. Matt. 5:1–7:29, John 13:34.

to find a better than a worse. Why should we doubt that a good way of punishing crimes is the one which we know long found favor of old with the Romans,[59] the greatest experts in managing the commonwealth? When men were convicted of atrocious crimes they condemned them for life to stone quarries and to digging in metal mines, and kept them constantly in chains.

" 'Yet, as concerns this matter, I can find no better system in any country than that which, in the course of my travels, I observed in Persia among the people commonly called the Polylerites,[60] a nation that is large and well-governed and, except that it pays an annual tribute to the Persian padishah, otherwise free and autonomous in its laws. They are far from the sea, almost ringed round by mountains, and satisfied with the products of their own land, which is in no way infertile. In consequence they rarely pay visits to other countries or receive them. In accordance with their long-standing national policy, they do not try to enlarge their territory and easily protect what they have from all aggression by their mountains and by the tribute paid to their overlord. Being completely free from militarism, they live a life more comfortable than splendid and more happy than renowned or famous, for even their name, I think, is hardly known except to their immediate neighbors.

" 'Now, in their land, persons who are convicted of theft repay to the owner what they have taken from him, not, as is usual elsewhere, to the prince, who, they consider, has as little right to the thing stolen as the thief himself.[61] But if the object is lost, the value is made up out of the thieves' goods, and the balance is then paid

59. See Aulus Gellius' interesting summary of punishments for theft (*NA* 11.18).
60. 'The People of Much Nonsense.'
61. Erasmus condemns the same abuse (*Prince*, p. 229).

intact to their wives and children. They themselves are condemned to hard labor.[62] Unless the theft is outrageous, they neither are confined to prison nor wear shackles about their feet but, without any bonds or restraints, are set to public works. Convicts who refuse to labor or are slack are not put in chains but urged on by the lash. If they do a good day's work, they need fear no insult or injury. The only check is that every night, after their names are called over, they are locked in their sleeping quarters.

" 'Except for the constant toil, their life has no hardship. For example, as serviceable to the common weal, they are fed well at the public's expense, the mode varying from place to place. In some parts, what is spent on them is raised by almsgiving. Though this method is precarious, the Polylerite people are so kindhearted that no other is found to supply the need more plentifully. In other parts, fixed public revenues are set aside to defray the cost. Elsewhere, all pay a specified personal tax for these purposes. Yes, and in some localities the convicts do no work for the community, but, whenever a private person needs a hired laborer, he secures in the market place a convict's service for that day at a fixed wage, a bit lower than what he would have paid for free labor. Moreover, the employer is permitted to chastise with stripes a hired man if he be lazy. The result is that they are never out of work and that each one, besides earning his own living, brings in something every day to the public treasury.

" 'All of them wear clothes of a color not worn by anyone else. Their hair is not shaved but cropped a little above the ears, from one of which the tip is cut off. Food and drink and clothes of the proper color may be given them by their friends. The gift of money is a capital

62. The Utopian penal system has much in common with the Polylerite, e.g. the hope of freedom.

offense, both for the donor and the receiver. It is no less dangerous for a free man to receive a penny for any reason from a condemned person, or for slaves (which is the name borne by the convicts) to touch weapons. The slaves of each district are distinguished by a special badge, which it is a capital offense to throw away, as it is to appear beyond their own bounds or to talk to a slave from another district. Further, it is no safer to plot escape than actually to run away. Yes, and the punishment for connivance in such a plan is death for the slave and slavery for the free man. On the other hand, rewards are appointed for an informer: money for a free man, liberty for a slave, and pardon and immunity for both for their complicity. The purpose is never to make it safer to follow out an evil plan than to repent of it.

" 'This is the law and this the procedure in the matter, as I have described it to you. You can easily see how humane and advantageous it is. The object of public anger is to destroy the vices but to save the persons and so to treat them that they necessarily become good and that, for the rest of their lives, they repair all the damage done before.

" 'Further, so little is it to be feared that they may sink back into their old evil ways, even travelers who have to go on a journey think themselves most safe if they secure as guides these slaves, who are changed with each new district. For the latter have nothing suitable with which to commit robbery. They bear no arms; money would merely insure the detection of the crime; punishment awaits the man who is caught; and there is absolutely no hope of escaping to a safe place. How could a man so cover his flight as to elude observation when he resembles ordinary people in no part of his attire—unless he were to run away naked? Even then his ear would betray him in his flight!

" 'But, of course, would there not at least be risk of

their taking counsel together and conspiring against the commonwealth? As if any district could conceive a hope of success without having first sounded and seduced the slave gangs of many other districts! The latter are so little able to conspire together that they may not even meet and converse or greet one another. Much less will they boldly divulge to their own fellow slaves the plot, which they know is dangerous to those concealing it and very profitable to those betraying it. On the other hand, no one is quite without hope of gaining his freedom eventually if he accepts his punishment in a spirit of obedience and resignation and gives evidence of reforming his future life; indeed, every year a number of them are granted their liberty which they have merited by their submissive behavior.'

"When I had finished this speech, I added that I saw no reason why this method might not be adopted even in England and be far more beneficial in its working than the justice which my legal opponent had praised so highly. The lawyer replied: 'Never could that system be established in England without involving the commonwealth in a very serious crisis.' In the act of making this statement, he shook his head and made a wry face and so fell silent. And all who were present gave him their assent.

"Then the Cardinal remarked: 'It is not easy to guess whether it would turn out well or ill inasmuch as absolutely no experiment has been made. If, after pronouncement of the sentence of death, the king were to order the postponement of its execution and, after limitation of the privileges of sanctuary,[63] were to try this system, then, if success proved its usefulness, it would be right to make the system law. In case of failure, then and

63. Already regulated by Innocent VIII in 1487. The sanctuary at Westminster is a setting in More's *Richard III* (*Comp. Works,* 2, 21 f.).

there to put to death those previously condemned would be no less for the public good and no more unjust than if execution were done here and now. In the meantime no danger can come of the experiment. Furthermore, I am sure that vagrants might very well be treated in the same way for, in spite of repeated legislation against them, we have made no progress.'

"When the Cardinal had finished speaking, they all vied in praising what they all had received with contempt when suggested by me, but especially the part relating to vagrants because this was the Cardinal's addition.[64]

"I am at a loss as to whether it were better to suppress what followed next, for it was quite absurd.[65] But I shall relate it since it was not evil in itself and had some bearing on the matter in question.

"There happened to be present a hanger-on, who wanted to give the impression of imitating a jester but whose imitation was too close to the real thing. His ill-timed witticisms were meant to raise a laugh, but he himself was more often the object of laughter than his jests. The fellow, however, sometimes let fall observations which were to the point, thus proving the proverb true, that if a man throws the dice often he will sooner or later make a lucky throw.[66] One of the guests happened to say:

" 'Raphael's proposal has made good provision for thieves. The Cardinal has taken precautions also for vagrants. It only remains now that public measures be devised for persons whom sickness or old age has brought to want and made unable to work for their living.'

---

64. For a similar anecdote concerning the flattery of Wolsey, see *Works*, pp. 1221–22, and Harpsfield, pp. 35–38.

65. The anecdote was included on the advice of More's friends (cf. Eras. *Ep.*, *4*, 224).

66. Cic. *Div.* 2.59.121; Eras. *Adag.* 113, 209.

" 'Give me leave,' volunteered the hanger-on. 'I shall see that this situation, too, be set right. I am exceedingly anxious to get this sort of person out of my sight. They have often harassed me with their pitiful whinings in begging for money—though they never could pitch a tune which would get a coin out of my pocket. For one of two things always happens: either I do not want to give or I cannot, since I have nothing to give. Now they have begun to be wise. When they see me pass by, they say nothing and spare their pains. They no longer expect anything from me—no more, by heaven, than if I were a secular priest! [67] As for me, I should have a law passed that all those beggars be distributed and divided among the Benedictine monasteries and that the men be made so-called lay brothers. The women I should order to become nuns.'

"The Cardinal smiled and passed it off in jest, but the rest took it in earnest. Now a certain theologian who was a friar[68] was so delighted by this jest at the expense of secular priests and of monks that he also began to make merry, though generally he was serious almost to the point of being dour.

" 'Nay,' said he, 'not even so will you be rid of mendicants unless you make provision for us friars too.'

" 'But this has been taken care of already,' retorted the hanger-on. 'His Eminence made excellent provision for you when he determined that tramps should be confined and made to work, for you are the worst tramps of all.'

67. Possibly alluding to Luke 10:31 (the priest in the story of the good Samaritan).

68. Cf. Eras. *Folly,* pp. 77–93, on theologians and monks. The friars were members of the mendicant orders (Augustinian, Carmelite, Dominican, or Franciscan), who originally traveled about, preaching the Gospel and living off alms. Hence the later reference to them as "tramps."

Book I

"When the company, looking at the Cardinal, saw that he did not think this jest any more amiss than the other, they all proceeded to take it up with vigor—but not the friar. He—and I do not wonder—deluged by these taunts, began to be so furious and enraged that he could not hold back even from abusing the joker. He called him a rascal, a slanderer, and a 'son of perdition,' quoting the while terrible denunciations out of Holy Scripture. Now the scoffer began to scoff in earnest and was quite in his element:

" 'Be not angry, good friar. It is written: "In your patience shall you possess your souls." ' [69]

"Then the friar rejoined—I shall repeat his very words: 'I am not angry, you gallows bird, or at least I do not sin, for the psalmist says: "Be angry, and sin not." ' [70]

"At this point the Cardinal gently admonished the friar to calm his emotions, but he replied:

" 'No, my lord, I speak motivated only by a good zeal —as I should. For holy men have had a good zeal; wherefore Scripture says, "The zeal of Thy house has eaten me up," [71] and churches resound with the hymn:[72] "The mockers of Eliseus as he went up to the house of God felt the zeal of the baldhead"—just as this mocking, scorning, ribald fellow will perhaps feel it.'

" 'Maybe,' said the Cardinal, 'you behave with proper feeling, but I think that you would act, if not more holily, at any rate more wisely, if you would not set your wits against those of a silly fellow and provoke a foolish duel with a fool.'

69. Luke 21:19.
70. Vulg. Ps. 4:5; Eph. 4:26.
71. Vulg. Ps. 68:10; cf. More, *Works*, p. 87.
72. Ascribed to Adam of St. Victor. The excited friar mistakenly uses *zelus* (pronounced at the time like *scelus*, 'crime') instead of the correct *zelum*, 'zeal'—an error which gives rise to a joke in the Latin original.

" 'No, my lord,' he replied, 'I should not do more wisely. Solomon himself, the wisest of men, says: "Answer a fool according to his folly" [73]—as I do now. I am showing him the pit into which he will fall if he does not take good heed, for, if many scorners of Eliseus, who numbered only one baldhead, felt the zeal of the baldhead, how much more will one scorner of many friars, among whom are numbered many baldheads! And, besides, we have a papal bull by which all who scoff at us are excommunicated!'

"When the Cardinal realized there was no making an end, he sent away the hanger-on by a motion of his head and tactfully turned the conversation to another subject. Soon afterwards he rose from the table and, going to hear the petitions of his suitors, dismissed us.

"Look, my dear More, with how lengthy a tale I have burdened you. I should have been quite ashamed to protract it if you had not eagerly called for it and seemed to listen as if you did not want any part of the conversation to be left out. Though I ought to have related this conversation more concisely, still I felt bound to tell it to exhibit the attitude of those who had rejected what I had said first yet who, immediately afterward, when the Cardinal did not disapprove of it, also gave their approval, flattering him so much that they even smiled on and almost allowed in earnest the fancies of the hanger-on, which his master in jest did not reject. From this reaction you may judge what little regard courtiers would pay to me and my advice."

"To be sure, my dear Raphael," I commented, "you have given me great pleasure, for everything you have said has been both wise and witty. Besides, while listening to you, I felt not only as if I were at home in my native land but as if I were become a boy again, by

73. Prov. 26:5.

Book I

being pleasantly reminded of the very Cardinal in whose court I was brought up as a lad.[74] Since you are strongly devoted to his memory, you cannot believe how much more attached I feel to you on that account, attached exceedingly as I have been to you already. Even now, nevertheless, I cannot change my mind but must needs think that, if you could persuade yourself not to shun the courts of kings, you could do the greatest good to the common weal by your advice. The latter is the most important part of your duty as it is the duty of every good man. Your favorite author, Plato, is of opinion that commonwealths will finally be happy only if either philosophers become kings or kings turn to philosophy.[75] What a distant prospect of happiness there will be if philosophers will not condescend even to impart their counsel to kings!"

"They are not so ungracious," he rejoined, "that they would not gladly do it—in fact, many have already done it in published books[76]—if the rulers would be ready to take good advice. But, doubtless, Plato was right in foreseeing that if kings themselves did not turn to philosophy, they would never approve of the advice of real philosophers because they have been from their youth saturated and infected with wrong ideas. This truth he found from his own experience with Dionysius.[77] If I proposed beneficial measures to some king and tried to uproot from his soul the seeds of evil and corruption, do

74. More later defends this practice (*Works*, p. 895).

75. Pl. *Rep.* 5.473 (cf. *Ep.* 7.326, 328), quoted ceaselessly throughout the Renaissance.

76. Political treatises by Plato, Aristotle, Isocrates, Plutarch, Xenophon, and Cicero in antiquity; by John of Salisbury, Thomas Aquinas, and Aegidius Romanus in the Middle Ages; and by Pontano, Clichtove, Budé, Erasmus, etc., in the Renaissance.

77. Treated with discourtesy, Plato became virtually a prisoner and even feared for his life (cf. Pl. *Ep.* 7–8; Nep. *Dion* 10.2.1–10.3.3; Plut. *Dion* 4.1–5.3, 10.1–20.2).

you not suppose that I should be forthwith banished or treated with ridicule?

"Come now, suppose I were at the court of the French king[78] and sitting in his privy council. In a most secret meeting, a circle of his most astute councilors over which he personally presides is setting its wits to work to consider by what crafty machinations he may keep his hold on Milan[79] and bring back into his power the Naples[80] which has been eluding his grasp; then overwhelm Venice[81] and subjugate the whole of Italy; next bring under his sway Flanders, Brabant,[82] and finally, the whole of Burgundy[83]—and other nations, too, whose territory he has already conceived the idea of usurping.

"At this meeting, one advises that a treaty should be made with the Venetians to last just as long as the king will find it convenient, that he should communicate his intentions to them, and that he should even deposit in their keeping part of the booty,[84] which, when all has gone according to his mind, he may reclaim. Another recommends the hiring of German *Landsknechte*,[85] and

78. Francis I, pursuing the policies of his predecessors, Charles VIII and Louis XII.

79. Seized by Louis XII in 1499, relinquished in 1512, regained by Francis I in September 1515, captured by Maximilian for one day only, March 25, 1516.

80. Captured by Charles VIII in 1495 and lost in 1496, recaptured by Louis XII in 1501 and yielded in 1504.

81. Defeated by Louis XII at the Battle of Agnadello (1509), but allied with Francis I in his invasion of Italy (1515).

82. Flanders was nominally a fief of the King of France but actually ruled by the House of Burgundy; Brabant had been controlled by the House of Burgundy since 1430.

83. Duchy annexed by Louis XI in 1477; county (Franche-Comté) seized by Louis XI in 1477 but returned by Charles VIII in 1493 to Maximilian's daughter Margaret, who became regent for life.

84. As a result of Francis I's victory at Marignano (September 1515), Venice regained Verona and the greater portion of the Lombard plain.

85. Infantry improved by Maximilian on the model of the Swiss.

another the mollification of the Swiss[86] with money, and another the propitiation of the offended majesty of the emperor[87] with gold as an acceptable offering. Another thinks that a settlement should be made with the King of Aragon[88] and that, as a guarantee of peace, someone else's kingdom of Navarre[89] should be ceded him! Another proposes that the Prince of Castile be caught by the prospect of a marriage alliance[90] and that some nobles of his court be drawn to the French side by a fixed pension.

"Meanwhile the most perplexing question of all comes up: what is to be done with England? [91] They agree that negotiations for peace should be undertaken, that an alliance always weak at best should be strengthened with the strongest bonds, and that the English should be called friends but suspected as enemies. The Scots[92] therefore must be posted in readiness, prepared for any opportunity to be let loose on the English if they make the slightest movement. Moreover, some exiled noble[93]

86. The most formidable mercenaries in Europe, but finally matched by the French at Marignano.

87. Maximilian, almost always in financial straits, was forced to leave Italy forever in 1516 after a mutiny of his unpaid troops.

88. Ferdinand, King of Aragon (1474–1516), regent of Castile (1504–16).

89. Conquered in 1512 and annexed to Castile in 1515 by Ferdinand through claims of his second wife, Germaine de Foix, against the actual ruler, John d'Albret, who was supported by France.

90. By the Treaty of Paris (March 24, 1515), Charles was to marry Louis XII's daughter, Renée; but by the Treaty of Noyon (August 13, 1516), he was to wed Francis I's infant daughter, Louise.

91. Francis I renewed the treaty with England (April 5, 1515) and began negotiations for a new treaty immediately after Noyon.

92. The Duke of Albany, heir of the infant James V, returned to Scotland in 1515, allegedly abetted by the French, and was declared regent.

93. Especially Richard de la Pole (*LP*, 2, Nos. 609, 1973), who had actually been recognized by Louis XII as King of England in 1512.

must be fostered secretly—for treaties prevent it being done openly—to maintain a claim to the throne, that by this handle France may keep in check a king in whom it has no confidence.

"In such a meeting, I say, when such efforts are being made, when so many distinguished persons are vying with each other in proposals of a warlike nature, what if an insignificant fellow like myself were to get up and advise going on another tack? Suppose I expressed the opinion that Italy should be left alone. Suppose I argued that we should stay at home because the single kingdom of France by itself was almost too large to be governed well by a single man so that the king should not dream of adding other dominions under his sway.[94] Suppose, then, I put before them the decisions made by the people called the Achorians[95] who live on the mainland to the south-southeast of the island of Utopia.

"Once upon a time they had gone to war to win for their king another kingdom to which he claimed to be the rightful heir by virtue of an old tie by marriage. After they had secured it, they saw they would have no less trouble in keeping it than they had suffered in obtaining it. The seeds of rebellion from within or of invasion from without were always springing up in the people thus acquired. They realized they would have to fight constantly for them or against them and to keep an army in continual readiness. In the meantime they were being plundered, their money was being taken out of the country, they were shedding their blood for the little glory of someone else, peace was no more secure than before, their morals at home were being corrupted by war, the lust for robbery was becoming second nature,

94. Cf. More's "On the Lust for Power" (*Epigr.*, pp. 218–19).

95. 'Without place, region, district.' The direction (southeast) points to France. The whole anecdote is a prophecy about French fortunes in Italy.

criminal recklessness was emboldened by killings in war, and the laws were held in contempt—all because the king, being distracted with the charge of two kingdoms, could not properly attend to either.

"At length, seeing that in no other way would there be any end to all this mischief, they took counsel together and most courteously offered their king his choice of retaining whichever of the two kingdoms he preferred. He could not keep both because there were too many of them to be ruled by half a king, just as no one would care to engage even a muleteer whom he had to share with someone else. The worthy king was obliged to be content with his own realm and to turn over the new one to one of his friends, who was driven out soon afterwards.

"Furthermore, suppose I proved that all this war-mongering, by which so many nations were kept in a turmoil on the French king's account, would, after draining his resources and destroying his people, at length by some mischance end in naught and that therefore he had better look after his ancestral kingdom and make it as prosperous and flourishing as possible,[96] love his subjects and be loved by them, live with them and rule them gently, and have no designs upon other kingdoms since what he already possessed was more than enough for him. What reception from my listeners, my dear More, do you think this speech of mine would find?"

"To be sure, not a very favorable one," I granted.

"Well, then, let us proceed," he continued. "Picture the councilors of some king or other debating with him and devising by what schemes they may heap up treasure for him.[97] One advises crying up the value of money

96. Cf. Erasmus' famous *Adag.* 1401: "You have obtained Sparta —now adorn her."

97. The best commentaries on this whole council are Erasmus' *Prince* for humanistic theory and Bacon's *Henry VII* for actual practice.

when he has to pay any and crying down its value below the just rate when he has to receive any—with the double result that he may discharge a large debt with a small sum and, when only a small sum is due to him, may receive a large one. Another suggests a make-believe war under pretext of which he would raise money and then, when he saw fit, make peace with solemn ceremonies to throw dust in his simple people's eyes because their loving monarch in compassion would fain avoid human bloodshed.

"Another councilor reminds him of certain old and moth-eaten laws, annulled by long non-enforcement, which no one remembers being made and therefore everyone has transgressed. The king should exact fines for their transgression, there being no richer source of profit nor any more honorable than such as has an out-ward mask of justice! Another recommends that under heavy penalties he prohibit many things and especially such as it is to the people's advantage not to allow. After-wards for money he should give a dispensation to those with whose interests the prohibition has interfered. Thus favor is won with the people and a double profit is made: first, by exacting fines from those whose greed of gain has entangled them in the snare and, second, by selling privileges to others—and, to be sure, the higher the price the better the king, since he hates to give any private citizen a privilege which is contrary to the public welfare and will not do so except at a great price!

"Another persuades him that he must bind to himself the judges, who will in every case decide in favor of the king's side. In addition, he must summon them to the palace and invite them to debate his affairs in his pres-ence. There will be no cause of his so patently unjust in which one of them will not, either from a desire to contradict or from shame at repeating another's view or to curry favor, find some loophole whereby the law can be perverted. When through the opposite opinions of the judges a thing in itself as clear as daylight has been made a subject of debate, and when truth has become a matter of doubt, the king is opportunely furnished a handle to interpret the law in his own interest. Everyone else will acquiesce from shame or from fear. Afterwards the decision is boldly pronounced from the Bench. Then, too, a pretext can never be wanting for deciding on the king's side. For such a judge it is enough that either equity be on his side or the letter of the law or the twisted meaning of the written word or, what finally outweighs all law with conscientious judges, the indisputable royal prerogative!

"All the councilors agree and consent to the famous statement of Crassus:[98] no amount of gold is enough for the ruler who has to keep an army. Further, the king, however much he wishes, can do no wrong; for all that all men possess is his, as they themselves are, and so much is a man's own as the king's kindness has not taken away from him. It is much to the king's interest that the latter be as little as possible, seeing that his safeguard lies in the fact that the people do not grow insolent with wealth and freedom. These things make them less patient to endure harsh and unjust commands, while, on the other hand, poverty and need blunt their spirits, make them patient, and take away from the oppressed the lofty spirit of rebellion.[99]

"At this point, suppose I were again to rise and maintain that these counsels are both dishonorable and dangerous for the king, whose very safety, not merely his honor, rests on the people's resources rather than his own. Suppose I should show that they choose a king for

98. Cic. *Off.* 1.8.25.
99. Cf. Arist. *Pol.* 5.9.4, 1313b, and Bacon's *Henry VII*, p. 237.

their own sake and not for his[100]—to be plain, that by his labor and effort they may live well and safe from injustice and wrong. For this very reason, it belongs to the king to take more care for the welfare of his people than for his own, just as it is the duty of a shepherd, insofar as he is a shepherd, to feed his sheep rather than himself.[101]

"The blunt facts reveal that they are completely wrong in thinking that the poverty of the people is the safeguard of peace. Where will you find more quarreling than among beggars? Who is more eager for revolution than he who is discontented with his present state of life? Who is more reckless in the endeavor to upset everything, in the hope of getting profit from some source or other, than he who has nothing to lose? Now if there were any king who was either so despicable or so hateful to his subjects[102] that he could not keep them in subjection otherwise than by ill usage, plundering, and confiscation and by reducing them to beggary, it would surely be better for him to resign his throne than to keep it by such means—means by which, though he retain the name of authority, he loses its majesty. It is not consistent with the dignity of a king to exercise authority over beggars but over prosperous and happy subjects. This was certainly the sentiment of that noble and lofty spirit,

100. "A governor of people is made for the people, and not the people for the governor" (More, *Works*, p. 373). Cf. More's *Epigr.*, Nos. 1, 91–94, 96–97, 102–03, 182, 227. Aristotle's distinction between a king and a tyrant (*Pol.* 4.8.3, 1295a) was echoed constantly through the Middle Ages and the Renaissance.

101. The figure, used also by More as Chancellor at the opening of Parliament in 1529, occurs everywhere, e.g., Ezek. 34:2, Jer. 23:1; Hom. *Il.* 2.243, 4.296, and passim; Pl. *Rep.* 1.345; Arist. *Eth. Nic.* 8.11.1, 1161a; and Dio Chrys. *Or.* 1.13, 1.17, 1.28, 2.6, 4.43–44.

102. Hatred and contempt play "the greatest roles in the overthrow of empire" (Arist. *Pol.* 5.8.14–20, 1311b–12b).

46

Fabricius,[103] who replied that he would rather be a ruler
of rich people than be rich himself.

"To be sure, to have a single person enjoy a life of
pleasure and self-indulgence amid the groans and lamen-
tations of all around him is to be the keeper,[104] not of
a kingdom, but of a jail. In fine, as he is an incompetent
physician who cannot cure one disease except by creating
another, so he who cannot reform the lives of citizens in
any other way than by depriving them of the good
things of life must admit that he does not know how to
rule free men.[105]

"Yea, the king had better amend his own indolence or
arrogance, for these two vices generally cause his people
either to despise him or to hate him. Let him live harm-
lessly on what is his own. Let him adjust his expenses
to his revenues. Let him check mischief and crime, and,
by training his subjects rightly, let him prevent rather
than allow the spread of activities which he will have to
punish afterwards. Let him not be hasty in enforcing
laws fallen into disuse, especially those which, long given
up, have never been missed. Let him never take in
compensation for violation anything that a private person would be forbidden in court to appropriate for the
reason that such would be an act of crooked craftiness.

"What if then I were to put before them the law of the
Macarians,[106] a people not very far distant from Utopia?

103. Attributed to Gaius Fabricius Luscinus, Roman commander
against Pyrrhus of Epirus in 278 B.C., by Frontinus and Aulus
Gellius, but to Manius Curius Dentatus, victor over the Samnites
and over Pyrrhus at Beneventum, by Cicero, Pliny, Athenaeus, and
Plutarch.

104. Probably intended to recall the Guardian in Plato's *Republic*.

105. Cf. Xen. *Oec.* 21.12; Arist. *Pol.* 1.5.1–2, 1259a–b; Erasmus,
Prince, pp. 133, 170, 179–80.

106. 'The Happy, Blessed Ones.'

Their king, on the day he first enters into office, is bound by an oath at solemn sacrifices that he will never have at one time in his coffer more than a thousand pounds of gold or its equivalent in silver.[107] They report that this law was instituted by a very good king, who cared more for his country's interest than his own wealth, to be a barrier against hoarding so much money as would cause a lack of it among his people. He saw that this treasure would be sufficient for the king to put down rebellion and for his kingdom to meet hostile invasions. It was not large enough, however, to tempt him to encroach on the possessions of others. The prevention of the latter was the primary purpose of his legislation. His secondary consideration was that provision was thus made to forestall any shortage of the money needed in the daily business transactions of the citizens. He felt, too, that since the king had to pay out whatever came into his treasury beyond the limit prescribed by law, he would not seek occasion to commit injustice. Such a king will be both a terror to the evil and beloved by the good. To sum it all up, if I tried to obtrude these and like ideas on men strongly inclined to the opposite way of thinking, to what deaf ears should I tell the tale!"

"Deaf indeed, without doubt," I agreed, "and, by heaven, I am not surprised. Neither, to tell the truth, do I think that such ideas should be thrust on people, or such advice given, as you are positive will never be listened to. What good could such novel ideas do, or how could they enter the minds of individuals who are already taken up and possessed by the opposite conviction? In the private conversation of close friends this academic philosophy is not without its charm, but in

107. At his death, Henry VII was rumored to have £1,800,000, "a huge Masse of Money, even for these times" (Bacon, *Henry VII*, p. 230).

the councils of kings, where great matters are debated with great authority, there is no room for these notions."

"That is just what I meant," he rejoined, "by saying there is no room for philosophy with rulers."

"Right," I declared, "that is true—not for this academic[108] philosophy which thinks that everything is suitable to every place. But there is another philosophy, more practical for statesmen, which knows its stage, adapts itself to the play in hand, and performs its role neatly and appropriately. This is the philosophy which you must employ. Otherwise we have the situation in which a comedy of Plautus[109] is being performed and the household slaves are making trivial jokes at one another and then you come on the stage in a philosopher's attire and recite the passage from the *Octavia*[110] where Seneca is disputing with Nero. Would it not have been preferable to take a part without words than by reciting something inappropriate to make a hodgepodge of comedy and tragedy? You would have spoiled and upset the actual play by bringing in irrelevant matter—even if your contribution would have been superior in itself. Whatever play is being performed, perform it as best you can, and do not upset it all simply because you think of another which has more interest.

"So it is in the commonwealth. So it is in the deliberations of monarchs. If you cannot pluck up wrongheaded opinions by the root, if you cannot cure according to your heart's desire vices of long standing, yet you must not on that account desert the commonwealth. You

108. *scholastica*, i.e. characteristic of the Schoolmen (or of the universities, which they still controlled for the most part), not necessarily in a pejorative sense; contrasted with *ciuilior*, i.e. better befitting citizens or statesmen.

109. Cf. *Aul.* 2.4–9.280–405, *Pers.* 5.1.753–77, *Stich.* 5.1–7.641–772.

110. A tragedy doubtfully attributed to Seneca: cf. especially ll. 378–592.

49

must not abandon the ship in a storm because you cannot control the winds.[111]

"On the other hand, you must not force upon people new and strange ideas which you realize will carry no weight with persons of opposite conviction. On the contrary, by the indirect approach you must seek and strive to the best of your power to handle matters tactfully. What you cannot turn to good you must at least make as little bad as you can. For it is impossible that all should be well unless all men were good, a situation which I do not expect for a great many years to come!" [112]

"By this approach," he commented, "I should accomplish nothing else than to share the madness of others as I tried to cure their lunacy. If I would stick to the truth, I must needs speak in the manner I have described. To speak falsehoods, for all I know, may be the part of a philosopher,[113] but it is certainly not for me. Although that speech of mine might perhaps be unwelcome and disagreeable to those councilors, yet I cannot see why it should seem odd even to the point of folly. What if I told them the kind of things which Plato creates in his republic or which the Utopians actually put in practice in theirs? Though such institutions were superior (as, to be sure, they are), yet they might appear odd because here individuals have the right of private property, there all things are common.

"To persons who had made up their minds to go headlong by the opposite road, the man who beckons them back and points out dangers ahead can hardly be wel-

111. Cf. Pl. *Rep.* 6.488A–89A; Dio Chrys. *Or.* 3.63–65, 4.25; and Erasmus, *Prince*, pp. 140, 184, 203–204, on the ship of state. More later uses the figure in depicting a pusillanimous bishop (*Works*, pp. 1371–72).

112. Cf. Erasmus: "It is too much even to hope that all men will be good" (*Prince*, p. 143).

113. Cf. Pl. *Rep.* 3.389, 3.414–15, 5.459, and Quint. *Inst.* 12.1.38. More declares himself not to be "scrupulously truthful" (*S.L.*, p. 65).

come. But, apart from this aspect, what did my speech contain that would not be appropriate or obligatory to have propounded everywhere? Truly, if all the things which by the perverse morals of men have come to seem odd are to be dropped as unusual and absurd, we must dissemble among Christians almost all the doctrines of Christ. Yet He forbade us to dissemble them to the extent that what He had whispered in the ears of His disciples He commanded to be preached openly from the house-tops.[114] The greater part of His teaching is far more different from the morals of mankind than was my discourse. But preachers, crafty men that they are, finding that men grievously disliked to have their morals adjusted to the rule of Christ and following I suppose your advice, accommodated His teaching to men's morals as if it were a rule of soft lead [115] that at least in some way or other the two might be made to correspond. By this method I cannot see what they have gained, except that men may be bad in greater comfort.

"And certainly I should make as little progress in the councils of princes. For I should hold either a different opinion, which would amount to having none at all, or else the same, and then I should, as Mitio says in Terence, help their madness.[116] As to that indirect approach of yours, I cannot see its relevancy; I mean your advice to use my endeavors, if all things cannot be made good, at least to handle them tactfully and, as far as one may, to make them as little bad as possible. At court there is no room for dissembling, nor may one shut one's eyes to things. One must openly approve the worst counsels and subscribe to the most ruinous

114. For Christ's advocacy of communism, see Eras. *Adag.* 1 and 3001. Cf. Matt. 10:27; Luke 12:3.

115. The Lesbian rule: cf. Arist. *Eth. Nic.* 5.10.7, 1137b; Eras. *Adag.* 493; More, *Works,* p. 152, and *S.L.,* p. 27.

116. Ter. *Ad.* 1.2.145–47.

decrees. He would be counted a spy and almost a traitor, who gives only faint praise to evil counsels.

"Moreover, there is no chance for you to do any good because you are brought among colleagues who would easily corrupt even the best of men before being reformed themselves. By their evil companionship, either you will be seduced yourself or, keeping your own integrity and innocence, you will be made a screen for the wickedness and folly of others. Thus you are far from being able to make anything better by that indirect approach of yours.

"For this reason, Plato by a very fine comparison shows why philosophers are right in abstaining from administration of the commonwealth. They observe the people rushing out into the streets and being soaked by constant showers and cannot induce them to go indoors and escape the rain. They know that, if they go out, they can do no good but will only get wet with the rest. Therefore, being content if they themselves at least are safe, they keep at home, since they cannot remedy the folly of others.[117]

"Yet surely, my dear More, to tell you candidly my heart's sentiments, it appears to me that wherever you have private property and all men measure all things by cash values,[118] there it is scarcely possible for a commonwealth to have justice or prosperity—unless you think justice exists where all the best things flow into the hands of the worst citizens or prosperity prevails where all is divided among very few—and even they are not altogether well off, while the rest are downright wretched.

117. Pl. *Rep.* 6.496; cf. More, *Corresp.*, pp. 512–13, 518–19.
118. An adaptation of Aristotle's definition of money (*Eth. Nic.* 4.1.1, 1119b; 5.5.10, 1133a; 9.1.2, 1164a). Cf. Eccles. 10:19; Erasmus, *Folly*, p. 104.

Book 1

"As a result, when in my heart I ponder on the extremely wise and holy institutions of the Utopians, among whom, with very few laws, affairs are ordered so aptly that virtue has its reward, and yet, with equality of distribution, all men have abundance of all things, and then when I contrast with their policies the many nations elsewhere ever making ordinances and yet never one of them achieving good order—nations where whatever a man has acquired he calls his own private property, but where all these laws daily framed are not enough for a man to secure or to defend or even to distinguish from someone else's the goods which each in turn calls his own, a predicament readily attested by the numberless and ever new and interminable lawsuits—when I consider, I repeat, all these facts, I become more partial to Plato and less surprised at his refusal to make laws for those who rejected that legislation which gave to all an equal share in all goods.

"This wise sage, to be sure, easily foresaw that the one and only road to the general welfare lies in the maintenance of equality in all respects. I have my doubts that the latter could ever be preserved where the individual's possessions are his private property. When every man aims at absolute ownership of all the property he can get, be there never so great abundance of goods, it is all shared by a handful who leave the rest in poverty. It generally happens that the one class preeminently deserves the lot of the other, for the rich are greedy, unscrupulous, and useless, while the poor are well-behaved, simple, and by their daily industry more beneficial to the commonwealth than to themselves. I am fully persuaded that no just and even distribution of goods can be made and that no happiness can be found in human affairs unless private property is utterly abolished. While it lasts, there will always remain a heavy and inescapable burden of poverty and misfortunes for by far the greatest and by far the best part of mankind.

"I admit that this burden can be lightened to some extent, but I contend that it cannot be removed entirely. A statute might be made that no person should hold more than a certain amount of land and that no person should have a monetary income beyond that permitted by law. Special legislation might be passed to prevent the monarch from being overmighty and the people overweening; likewise, that public offices should not be solicited with gifts, nor be put up for sale, nor require lavish personal expenditures.[119] Otherwise, there arise, first, the temptation to recoup one's expenses by acts of fraud and plunder and, secondly, the necessity of appointing rich men to offices which ought rather to have been administered by wise men. By this type of legislation, I maintain, as sick bodies which are past cure can be kept up by repeated medical treatments, so these evils, too, can be alleviated and made less acute. There is no hope, however, of a cure and a return to a healthy condition as long as each individual is master of his own property. Nay, while you are intent upon the cure of one part, you make worse the malady of the other parts. Thus, the healing of the one member reciprocally breeds the disease of the other as long as nothing can so be added to one as not to be taken away from another." [120]

"But," I ventured, "I am of the contrary opinion.[121]

119. Cf. Arist. *Pol.* 2.8.7, 1273b; Erasmus, *Prince*, pp. 236–37; More, *Epigr.*, p. 141; and Stapleton, p. 88.

120. On the care of "the whole body politic," not of single members, cf. Pl. *Rep.* 4.420B, 5.462D–E; Cic. *Off.* 1.25.85; and Erasmus, *Prince*, p. 205.

121. The traditional Aristotelico-Scholastic arguments follow: cf. Arist. *Pol.* 2.1.1–2.3.13, 1260b–66a; Aquinas, *Com. in Arist. Pol.* 2.1–7; Aeg. Rom. *Reg. prin.* 2.3.5–7, 3.1.9–11.

Book I

Life cannot be satisfactory where all things are common. How can there be a sufficient supply of goods when each withdraws himself from the labor of production? For the individual does not have the motive of personal gain and he is rendered slothful by trusting to the industry of others. Moreover, when people are goaded by want and yet the individual cannot legally keep as his own what he has gained, must there not be trouble from continual bloodshed and riot? This holds true especially since the authority of magistrates and respect for their office have been eliminated, for how there can be any place for these among men who are all on the same level I cannot even conceive."

"I do not wonder," he rejoined, "that it looks this way to you, being a person who has no picture at all, or else a false one, of the situation I mean. But you should have been with me in Utopia and personally seen their manners and customs as I did, for I lived there more than five years and would never have wished to leave except to make known that new world. In that case you unabashedly would admit that you had never seen a well-ordered people anywhere but there."

"Yet surely," objected Peter Giles, "it would be hard for you to convince me that a better-ordered people is to be found in that new world than in the one known to us. In the latter I imagine there are equally excellent minds, as well as commonwealths which are older than those in the new world. In these commonwealths long experience has come upon very many advantages for human life—not to mention also the chance discoveries made among us, which no human mind could have devised."

"As for the antiquity of commonwealths," he countered, "you could give a sounder opinion if you had read the historical accounts of that world. If we must believe them, there were cities among them before there were men among us. Furthermore, whatever either brains have invented or chance has discovered hitherto could have happened equally in both places. But I hold for certain that, even though we may surpass them in brains, we are far inferior to them in application and industry.

"According to their chronicles, up to the time of our landing they had never heard anything about our activities (they call us the Ultra-equinoctials) except that twelve hundred years ago[122] a ship driven by a tempest was wrecked on the island of Utopia. Some Romans and Egyptians[123] were cast on shore and remained on the island without ever leaving it. Now mark what good advantage their industry took of this one opportunity. The Roman empire possessed no art capable of any use which they did not either learn from the shipwrecked strangers or discover for themselves after receiving the hints for investigation—so great a gain was it to them that on a single occasion some persons were carried to their shores from ours.

"But if any like fortune has ever driven anyone from their shores to ours, the event is as completely forgotten as future generations will perhaps forget that I had once been there. And, just as they immediately at one meeting appropriated to themselves every good discovery of ours, so I suppose it will be long before we adopt anything that is better arranged with them than with us. This trait, I judge, is the chief reason why, though we are inferior to them neither in brains nor in resources, their commonwealth is more wisely governed and more happily flourishing than ours."

"If so, my dear Raphael," said I, "I beg and beseech you, give us a description of the island. Do not be brief, but set forth in order the terrain, the rivers, the cities, the inhabitants, the traditions, the customs, the laws,

122. The date has not been satisfactorily explained.
123. Traditionally the originators of philosophy, mathematics, etc.

and, in fact, everything which you think we should like to know. And you must think we wish to know everything of which we are still ignorant."

"There is nothing," he declared, "I shall be more pleased to do, for I have the facts ready to hand. But the description will take time."

"In that case," I suggested, "let us go in to dine. Afterwards we shall take up as much time as we like."

"Agreed," he replied.

So we went in and dined.[124] We then returned to the same place, sat down on the same bench, and gave orders to the servants that we should not be interrupted. Peter Giles and I urged Raphael to fulfill his promise. As for him, when he saw us intent and eager to listen, after sitting in silent thought for a time, he began his tale as follows.

THE END OF BOOK ONE.

BOOK TWO FOLLOWS.

---

124. In More's *Dialogue Concerning Heresies,* Bks. I and III end with dinner, and Bks. II and IV begin with a return to the garden after dinner.

THE BEST STATE OF A COMMONWEALTH, THE DISCOURSE OF RAPHAEL HYTHLODAEUS AS REPORTED BY THOMAS MORE, CITIZEN AND SHERIFF OF LONDON

BOOK II

The island[1] of the Utopians extends in the center (where it is broadest) for two hundred miles[2] and is not much narrower for the greater part of the island, but toward both ends it begins gradually to taper. These ends form a circle five hundred miles in circumference and so make the island look like a new moon, the horns of which are divided by straits about eleven miles across. The straits then unfold into a wide expanse. As the winds are kept off by the land which everywhere surrounds it, the bay is like a huge lake, smooth rather than rough, and thus converts almost the whole center of the country into a harbor which lets ships cross in every direction to the great convenience of the inhabitants.

The mouth of this bay is rendered perilous here by shallows and there by reefs. Almost in the center of the gap stands one great crag which, being visible, is not dangerous. A tower built on it is occupied by a

1. In Utopia, More "represented chiefly Britain," according to Erasmus (*Ep.*, *4*, 21).

2. The breadth of England, according to the *Saint Albans Chronicle* (London, 1515), sig. A₂.

garrison. The other rocks are hidden and therefore treacherous. The channels are known only to the natives, and so it does not easily happen that any foreigner enters the bay except with a Utopian pilot. In fact, the entrance is hardly safe even for themselves, unless they guide themselves by landmarks on the shore. If these were removed to other positions, they could easily lure an enemy's fleet, however numerous, to destruction.

On the outer side of the island, harbors are many. Everywhere, however, the landing is so well defended by nature or by engineering that a few defenders can prevent strong forces from coming ashore.[3]

As the report goes and as the appearance of the ground shows, the island once was not surrounded by sea. But Utopus,[4] who as conqueror gave the island its name (up to then it had been called Abraxa)[5] and who brought the rude and rustic people to such a perfection of culture and humanity as makes them now superior to almost all other mortals, gained a victory at his very first landing. He then ordered the excavation of fifteen miles on the side where the land was connected with the continent and caused the sea to flow around the land.[6] He set to the task not only the natives but, to prevent them from thinking the labor a disgrace, his own soldiers also. With the work divided among so many hands, the enterprise was finished with incredible speed and struck the neighboring peoples, who at first had derided the project as vain, with wonder and terror at its success.

3. Cf. Arist. *Pol.* 7.5.2, 1236b–37a, and on England's vulnerability, Fortescue, *Gov.*, pp. 115, 118, 138, 282–83.

4. 'No place,' therefore, 'ruler over no place.'

5. Properly *Abraxas* (the component letters of which, according to the Greek system of numerals, total 365), the name given by Basilides the Gnostic to the highest of his 365 heavens.

6. On a similar achievement of Xerxes at Athos, see Hdt. 7.22–24, Strab. 7.331, Dio Chrys. *Or.* 3.31.

Book II

The island contains fifty-four city-states,[7] all spacious and magnificent, identical in language, traditions, customs, and laws. They are similar also in layout and everywhere, as far as the nature of the ground permits, similar even in appearance. None of them is separated by less than twenty-four miles from the nearest, but none is so isolated that a person cannot go from it to another in a day's journey on foot. From each city three old and experienced citizens meet to discuss the affairs of common interest to the island once a year at Amaurotum,[8] for this city, being in the very center of the country, is situated most conveniently for the representatives of all sections. It is considered the chief as well as the capital city.

The lands are so well assigned to the cities that each has at least twelve miles of country on every side, and on some sides even much more, to wit, the side on which the cities are farther apart. No city has any desire to extend its territory, for they consider themselves the tenants rather than the masters of what they hold.

Everywhere in the rural districts they have, at suitable distances from one another, farmhouses well equipped with agricultural implements.[9] They are inhabited by citizens who come in succession to live there. No rural household numbers less than forty men and women, besides two serfs attached to the soil. Over them are set a master and a mistress, serious in mind and ripe in years. Over every group of thirty households rules a phylarch.[10]

7. To reach fifty-four, Lupton (*Utopia*, p. 119, n. 1) adds the City of London to the fifty-three counties given in William Harrison's *Description of England* (1577).

8. 'Darkling City,' a term apt for foggy London.

9. Agriculture comes first because food ranks first among the state's needs (Arist. *Pol.* 7.7.4, 1328b).

10. 'The Head of a Tribe.'

61

Twenty from each household return every year to the city, namely, those having completed two years in the country. As substitutes in their place, the same number are sent from the city. They are to be trained by those who have been there a year and who therefore are more expert in farming; they themselves will teach others in the following years. There is thus no danger of anything going wrong with the annual food supply through want of skill, as might happen if all at one time were newcomers and novices at farming. Though this system of changing farmers is the rule, to prevent any individual's being forced against his will to continue too long in a life of rather hard work, yet many men who take a natural pleasure in agricultural pursuits obtain leave to stay several years.

The occupation of the farmers is to cultivate the soil, to feed the animals, and to get wood and convey it to the city either by land or by water, whichever way is more convenient. They breed a vast quantity of poultry by a wonderful contrivance. The hens do not brood over the eggs, but the farmers, by keeping a great number of them at a uniform heat, bring them to life and hatch them. As soon as they come out of the shell, the chicks follow and acknowledge humans as their mothers! [11]

They rear very few horses, and these only high-spirited ones, which they use for no other purpose than for exercising their young men in horsemanship. All the labor of cultivation and transportation is performed by oxen, which they admit are inferior to horses in a sudden spurt but which are far superior to them in staying power and endurance and not liable to as many diseases. Moreover, it requires less trouble and expense to feed them. When they are past work, they finally are of use for food.

11. Cf. Plin. *HN* 10.54–55 [75–76] and, on the following-instinct, W. James, *Principles of Psychology* (Chicago, 1952), pp. 708–10. More was a great fancier of birds and animals (Eras. *Ep.*, *4*, 16–17).

They sow grain only for bread.[12] Their drink is wine or cider or perry, or it is even water.[13] The latter is sometimes plain and often that in which they have boiled honey or licorice, whereof they have a great abundance.

Though they are more than sure how much food the city with its adjacent territory consumes, they produce far more grain and cattle than they require for their own use: they distribute the surplus among their neighbors. Whenever they need things not found in the country, they send for all the materials from the city and, having to give nothing in exchange, obtain it from the municipal officials without the bother of bargaining. For very many go there every single month to observe the holyday.

When the time of harvest is at hand, the agricultural phylarchs inform the municipal officials what number of citizens they require to be sent. The crowd of harvesters, coming promptly at the appointed time, dispatch the whole task of harvesting almost in a single day of fine weather.

THE CITIES, ESPECIALLY AMAUROTUM

The person who knows one of the cities will know them all, since they are exactly alike insofar as the terrain permits. I shall therefore picture one or other (nor does it matter which), but which should I describe rather than Amaurotum? First, none is worthier, the rest deferring to it as the meeting place of the national senate; and, secondly, none is better known to me, as being one in which I had lived for five whole years.

12. But not for beer or ale, for a commendation of which see Elyot's *Castell of Helth* (London, 1541), fol. 36^v. Cf. Tac. *Germ.* 23.

13. Eulogized by Elyot, *Helth*, fols. 33^v–34^v. On More's water-drinking see Harpsfield, p. 142; on Epicurus', Diog. Laert. 10.11.

To proceed. Amaurotum is situated on the gentle slope of a hill and is almost four-square in outline. Its breadth is about two miles starting just below the crest of the hill and running down to the river Anydrus;[1] its length along the river is somewhat more than its breadth.

The Anydrus rises eighty miles above Amaurotum from a spring not very large; but, being increased in size by several tributaries, two of which are of fair size, it is half a mile broad in front of the city. After soon becoming still broader and after running farther for sixty miles,[2] it falls into the ocean. Through the whole distance between the city and the sea, and even above the city for some miles, the tide alternately flows in for six whole hours and then ebbs with an equally speedy current. When the sea comes in, it fills the whole bed of the Anydrus with its water for a distance of thirty miles, driving the river back. At such times it turns the water salt for some distance farther, but above that point the river grows gradually fresh and passes the city uncontaminated. When the ebb comes, the fresh and pure water extends down almost to the mouth of the river.

The city is joined to the opposite bank of the river not by a bridge built on wooden pillars or piles but by one magnificently arched with stonework.[3] It is situated in the quarter which is farthest from the sea so that ships may pass along the whole of that side of the city without hindrance.

They have also another river,[4] not very large, but very

1. 'Waterless.' On desirable nearness to river or sea cf. Arist. *Pol.* 7.5.2–7, 1326b–27b, and Patrizi, *Rep.* 7.12.

2. The Thames "doth twise ebbe and flowe more then lx. miles" within twenty-four hours (Vergil, *Eng. Hist., 1, 3*).

3. London Bridge.

4. Possibly the Fleet River.

Book II

gentle and pleasant, which rises out of the same hill whereon the city is built and runs down through its middle into the river Anydrus. The head and source of this river just outside the city has been connected with it by outworks, lest in case of hostile attack the water might be cut off and diverted or polluted.[5] From this point the water is distributed by conduits made of baked clay into various parts of the lower town. Where the ground makes that course impossible, the rain water collected in capacious cisterns is just as useful.

The city is surrounded by a high and broad wall with towers and ravelins at frequent intervals. A moat, dry but deep and wide and made impassable by thorn hedges, surrounds the fortifications on three sides; on the fourth the river itself takes the place of the moat.

The streets are well laid out both for traffic and for protection against the winds. The buildings, which are far from mean, are set together in a long row, continuous through the block and faced by a corresponding one. The house fronts of the respective blocks are divided by an avenue twenty feet broad. On the rear of the houses, through the whole length of the block, lies a broad garden enclosed on all sides by the backs of the blocks. Every home has not only a door into the street but a back door into the garden. What is more, folding doors, easily opened by hand and then closing of themselves, give admission to anyone. As a result, nothing is private property anywhere. Every ten years they actually exchange their very homes by lot.

The Utopians are very fond of their gardens.[6] In them they have vines, fruits, herbs, flowers, so well kept and flourishing that I never saw anything more fruitful and

5. Cf. Cyrus' capture of Babylon (Xen. *Cyr.* 7.5.15–34).

6. On the association of gardens with Epicurus and his followers cf. Patrizi, *Reg.* 3.8. On More's use of his own garden see Stapleton, p. 95.

more tasteful anywhere. Their zest in keeping them is increased not merely by the pleasure afforded them but by the keen competition between blocks as to which will have the best kept garden. Certainly you cannot readily find anything in the whole city more productive of profit and pleasure to the citizens. Therefore it would seem their founder attached the greatest importance to these gardens.

In fact, they report that the whole plan of the city had been sketched at the very beginning by Utopus himself. He left to posterity, however, to add the adornment and other improvements for which he saw one lifetime would hardly suffice. Their annals, embracing the history of 1760 years,[7] are preserved carefully and conscientiously in writing. Here they find stated that at first the houses were low, mere cabins and huts, haphazardly made with any wood to hand, with mud-plastered walls. They had thatched the ridged roofs with straw.

But now all the homes are of handsome appearance with three stories. The exposed faces of the walls are made of stone or cement or brick, rubble being used as filling for the empty space between the walls. The roofs are flat and covered with a kind of cement[8] which is cheap but so well mixed that it is impervious to fire and superior to lead in defying the damage caused by storms. They keep the winds out of their windows by glass (which is in very common use in Utopia) or sometimes by thin linen smeared with translucent oil or amber.[9] The advantage is twofold: the device results in letting more light in and keeping more wind out.

7. See R. J. Schoeck, "More, Plutarch, and King Agis," *Philological Quarterly*, 35 (1956), 366–75.

8. Possibly the "plaster of Paris" mentioned in Harrison's *Description of England*, according to Lupton (*Utopia*, p. 133, n. 1).

9. "Glass windows were . . . very scarce; lattice work, oiled linen, or horn were generally used" (*Relation of England*, p. 112, n. 71).

Book II

THE OFFICIALS

Every thirty families choose annually an official[1] whom in their ancient language they call a syphogrant[2] but in their newer a phylarch. Over ten syphogrants with their families is set a person once called a tranibor[3] but now a protophylarch.[4] The whole body of syphogrants, in number two hundred, having sworn to choose the man whom they judge most useful, by secret balloting appoint a governor, specifically one of the four candidates named to them by the people, for one is selected out of each of the four quarters of the city to be commended to the senate.

The governor holds office for life, unless ousted on suspicion of aiming at a tyranny. The tranibors are elected annually but are not changed without good reason. The other officials all hold their posts for one year.

The tranibors enter into consultation with the governor every other day and sometimes, if need arises, oftener. They take counsel about the commonwealth. If there are any disputes between private persons—there are very few—they settle them without loss of time. They always admit to the senate chamber two syphogrants, and different ones every day. It is provided that nothing concerning the commonwealth be ratified if it has not been discussed in the senate three days before the passing of the decree. To take counsel on matters of common interest outside the senate or the popular assembly is considered a capital offense. The object of these measures, they say, is to prevent it from being easy, by a conspiracy between the governor and the tranibors

1. Utopia is a representative democracy with free elections.
2. Derivation uncertain but possibly 'Wise Old Man' or, better, 'Silly Old Man.'
3. Derivation doubtful but possibly 'Plain Glutton.'
4. 'First among the Chiefs.'

and by tyrannous oppression of the people, to change the order of the commonwealth. Therefore whatever is considered important is laid before the assembly of the syphogrants who, after informing their groups of families, take counsel together and report their decision to the senate. Sometimes the matter is laid before the council of the whole island.

In addition, the senate has the custom of debating nothing on the same day on which it is first proposed but of putting it off till the next meeting. This is their rule lest anyone, after hastily blurting out the first thought that popped into his head, should afterwards give more thought to defending his opinion than to supporting what is for the good of the commonwealth, and should prefer to jeopardize the public welfare rather than to risk his reputation through a wrongheaded and misplaced shame, fearing he might be thought to have shown too little foresight at the first—though he should have been enough foresighted at the first to speak with prudence rather than with haste!

OCCUPATIONS

Agriculture is the one pursuit which is common to all, both men and women, without exception. They are all instructed in it from childhood,[1] partly by principles taught in school, partly by field trips to the farms closer to the city as if for recreation. Here they do not merely look on, but, as opportunity arises for bodily exercise, they do the actual work.

Besides agriculture[2] (which is, as I said, common to all), each is taught one particular craft as his own. This is generally either wool-working or linen-making or ma-

1. Cf. Pl. *Leg.* 1.643B–C.
2. A departure from Socrates' insistence upon a single occupation (*Rep.* 2.374B).

sonry or metal-working or carpentry. There is no other pursuit which occupies any number worth mentioning. As for clothes, these are of one and the same pattern throughout the island and down the centuries, though there is a distinction between the sexes and between the single and married. The garments are comely to the eye, convenient for bodily movement, and fit for wear in heat and cold. Each family, I say, does its own tailoring.

Of the other crafts, one is learned by each person, and not the men only, but the women too. The latter as the weaker sex have the lighter occupations[3] and generally work wool and flax. To the men are committed the remaining more laborious crafts. For the most part, each is brought up in his father's craft, for which most have a natural inclination. But if anyone is attracted to another occupation, he is transferred by adoption to a family pursuing that craft for which he has a liking. Care is taken not only by his father but by the authorities, too, that he will be assigned to a grave and honorable householder. Moreover, if anyone after being thoroughly taught one craft desires another also, the same permission is given. Having acquired both, he practices his choice unless the city has more need of the one than of the other.

The chief and almost the only function of the syphogrants is to manage and provide that no one sit idle,[4] but that each apply himself industriously to his trade, and yet that he be not wearied like a beast of burden with constant toil from early morning till late at night.[5] Such wretchedness is worse than the lot of slaves, and

3. Cf. Socrates' concession to women (*Rep.* 5.457A).

4. For More's view of sloth see *Works,* p. 1047.

5. Daybreak to nightfall during autumn and winter, 5:00 A.M. to between 7:00 and 8:00 P.M. in spring and summer (11° Hen. VII, 1495, c.22; 6° Hen. VIII, 1514–15, c.3).

yet it is almost everywhere the life of workingmen—
except for the Utopians. The latter divide the day and
night into twenty-four equal hours and assign only six
to work. There are three before noon, after which they
go to dinner. After dinner,[6] when they have rested for
two hours in the afternoon, they again give three to
work and finish up with supper. Counting one o'clock
as the first hour after noon, they go to bed about eight
o'clock, and sleep claims eight hours.[7]

The intervals between the hours of work, sleep, and
food are left to every man's discretion, not to waste in
revelry or idleness, but to devote the time free from
work to some other occupation according to taste. These
periods are commonly devoted to intellectual pursuits.
For it is their custom that public lectures are daily delivered in the hours before daybreak.[8] Attendance is
compulsory only for those who have been specially
chosen to devote themselves to learning. A great number
of all classes, however, both males and females,[9] flock
to hear the lectures, some to one and some to another,
according to their natural inclination. But if anyone
should prefer to devote this time to his trade, as is the
case with many minds which do not reach the level
for any of the higher intellectual disciplines, he is not
hindered; in fact, he is even praised as useful to the
commonwealth.

After supper they spend one hour in recreation, in
summer in the gardens, in winter in the common halls

6. Usually at 10:00 or 11:00 A.M. in England.

7. The Italian custom according to C. Heresbach, *De educandis
. . . principum liberis* (Torgau, 1598), Lib. I, Cap. 31. More slept
four or five hours (Stapleton, p. 31).

8. In Europe the first lecture was between 5:00 A.M. and 7:00
A.M., the hour varying with the university and with the season of
the year.

9. For More's views on the education of women, see Eras. *Ep., 4,*
577–79.

in which they have their meals.[10] There they either play music[11] or entertain themselves with conversation. Dice and that kind of foolish and ruinous game they are not acquainted with. They do play two games not unlike chess. The first[12] is a battle of numbers in which one number plunders another. The second[13] is a game in which the vices fight a pitched battle with the virtues. In the latter is exhibited very cleverly, to begin with, both the strife of the vices with one another and their concerted opposition to the virtues; then, what vices are opposed to what virtues, by what forces they assail them openly, by what stratagems they attack them indirectly, by what safeguards the virtues check the power of the vices, by what arts they frustrate their designs; and, finally, by what means the one side gains the victory.

But here, lest you be mistaken, there is one point you must examine more closely. Since they devote but six hours to work, you might possibly think the consequence to be some scarcity of necessities. But so far is this from being the case that the aforesaid time is not only enough but more than enough for a supply of all that is requisite for either the necessity or the convenience of living. This phenomenon you too will understand if you consider how large a part of the population in other countries exists without working. First, there are almost all the women, who constitute half the whole; or, where the women are busy, there as a rule the men are snoring in their stead. Besides, how great and how lazy is the crowd of priests and so-called

10. "For reste and recreacion shoulde bee but as a sauce" (More, *Works*, p. 1048).

11. On More's ability see Eras. *Ep.*, *4*, 15, and Stapleton, p. 15. For English pride in music see Erasmus, *Folly*, p. 61; and for humanistic attitudes see Patrizi, *Rep.* 2.2 and *Reg.* 2.15.

12. Such a game is described at the end of Jacques Lefèvre d'Étaples, *Arithmetica, etc.* (2d ed. Paris, 1514).

13. Elyot mentions a similar game in *Gou.* 1.26.

religious! [14] Add to them all the rich, especially the masters of estates, who are commonly termed gentlemen and noblemen. Reckon with them their retainers—I mean, that whole rabble of good-for-nothing swashbucklers. Finally, join in the lusty and sturdy beggars who make some disease an excuse for idleness. You will certainly find far less numerous than you had supposed those whose labor produces all the articles that mortals require for daily use.

Now estimate how few of those who do work are occupied in essential trades. For, in a society where we make money the standard of everything, it is necessary to practice many crafts which are quite vain and superfluous, ministering only to luxury and licentiousness. Suppose the host of those who now toil were distributed over only as few crafts as natural needs and conveniences require. In the great abundance of commodities which must then arise, the prices set on them would be too low for the craftsmen to earn their livelihood by their work. But suppose all those fellows who are now busied with unprofitable crafts, as well as all the lazy and idle throng, any one of whom now consumes as much of the fruits of other men's labors as any two of the workingmen, were all set to work and indeed to useful work. You can easily see how small an allowance of time would be enough and to spare for the production of all that is required by necessity or comfort (or even pleasure, provided it be genuine and natural). [15]

The very experience of Utopia makes the latter clear. In the whole city and its neighborhood, exemption from work is granted to hardly five hundred of the total of men and women whose age and strength make them fit

14. A typically humanistic qualification.
15. Anticipatory of the Utopian philosophy of pleasure.

for work.[16] Among them the syphogrants, though legally exempted from work, yet take no advantage of this privilege so that by their example they may the more readily attract the others to work. The same exemption is enjoyed by those whom the people, persuaded by the recommendation of the priests, have given perpetual freedom from labor through the secret vote of the syphogrants so that they may learn thoroughly the various branches of knowledge.[17] But if any of these scholars falsifies the hopes entertained of him, he is reduced to the rank of workingman. On the other hand, not seldom does it happen that a craftsman so industriously employs his spare hours on learning and makes such progress by his diligence that he is relieved of his manual labor and advanced into the class of men of learning. It is out of this company of scholars[18] that they choose ambassadors, priests, tranibors, and finally the governor himself, whom they call in their ancient tongue Barzanes[19] but in their more modern language Ademus.[20]

Nearly all the remaining populace being neither idle nor busied with useless occupations, it is easy to calculate how much good work can be produced in a very few hours. Besides the points mentioned, there is this further convenience that in most of the necessary crafts they do not require as much work as other nations. In the first place the erection or repair of buildings requires the constant labor of so many men elsewhere because what a father has built, his extravagant heir allows gradually to fall into ruin. As a result, what might have been kept up at small cost, his successor is obliged

16. Less than one-half of one per cent of the total population, i.e. less than five persons in a thousand.

17. A tribute to humanistic scholarship.

18. A qualification demanded by Socrates (Pl. *Rep.* 7.535B).

19. 'Son of Zeus.'

20. 'Peopleless.'

to erect anew at great expense. Further, often even when a house has cost one man a large sum, another is so fastidious that he thinks little of it. When it is neglected and therefore soon becomes dilapidated, he builds a second elsewhere at no less cost. But in the land of the Utopians, now that everything has been settled and the commonwealth established, a new home on a new site is a rare event, for not only do they promptly repair any damage, but they even take care to prevent damage. What is the result? With the minimum of labor, buildings last very long, and masons and carpenters sometimes have scarcely anything to do, except that they are set to hew out timber at home and to square and prepare stone meantime so that, if any work be required, a building may the sooner be erected.

In the matter of clothing, too, see how little toil and labor is needed. First, while at work, they are dressed unpretentiously in leather or hide, which lasts for seven years. When they go out in public, they put on a cape to hide their comparatively rough working clothes. This garment is of one color throughout the island and that the natural color. Consequently not only is much less woolen cloth needed than elsewhere, but what they have is much less expensive. On the other hand, since linen cloth is made with less labor, it is more used. In linen cloth only whiteness, in woolen cloth only cleanliness, is considered. No value is set on fineness of thread. So it comes about that, whereas elsewhere one man is not satisfied with four or five woolen coats of different colors and as many silk shirts, and the more fastidious not even with ten,[21] in Utopia a man is content with a single cape, lasting generally for two years. There is no reason, of course, why he should desire more, for if

21. For More's attitude see Eras. *Ep.*, *4*, 15. The acts passed against excess (1° Hen. VIII, 1509–10, c. 14; 6° Hen. VIII, 1514–15, c.1) apparently remained ineffective (More, *Works*, p. 993).

Book II

he had them he would not be better fortified against the cold nor appear better dressed in the least.

Wherefore, seeing that they are all busied with useful trades and are satisfied with fewer products from them, it even happens that when there is an abundance of all commodities, they sometimes take out a countless number of people to repair whatever public roads are in bad order. Often, too, when there is nothing even of this kind of work to be done, they announce publicly that there will be fewer hours of work. For the authorities do not keep the citizens against their will at superfluous labor since the constitution of their commonwealth looks in the first place to this sole object: that for all the citizens, as far as the public needs permit, as much time as possible should be withdrawn from the service of the body and devoted to the freedom and culture of the mind. It is in the latter that they deem the happiness of life to consist.

SOCIAL RELATIONS

But now, it seems, I must explain the behavior of the citizens toward one another, the nature of their social relations, and the method of distribution of goods. Since the city consists of households,[1] households as a rule are made up of those related by blood. Girls, upon reaching womanhood and upon being settled in marriage, go to their husbands' domiciles. On the other hand, male children and then grandchildren remain in the family and are subject to the oldest parent, unless he has become a dotard with old age. In the latter case the next oldest is put in his place.

But that the city neither be depopulated nor grow beyond measure, provision is made that no household

1. The exaltation of the family as the foundation of the state marks a radical difference between *Utopia* and Plato's *Republic*.

shall have fewer than ten or more than sixteen adults; there are six thousand [2] such households in each city, apart from its surrounding territory. Of children under age,[3] of course, no number can be fixed. This limit is easily observed by transferring those who exceed the number in larger families into those that are under the prescribed number. Whenever all the families of a city reach their full quota, the extra persons help to make up the deficient population of other cities.

And if the population throughout the island should happen to swell above the fixed quotas, they enroll citizens out of every city and, on the mainland nearest them, wherever the natives have much unoccupied and uncultivated land, they found a colony under their own laws. They join with themselves the natives if they are willing to dwell with them. When such a union takes place, the two parties gradually and easily merge and together absorb the same way of life and the same customs, much to the great advantage of both peoples. By their procedures they make the land sufficient for both, which previously seemed poor and barren to the natives. The inhabitants who refuse to live according to their laws, they drive from the territory which they carve out for themselves. If they resist, they wage war against them. They consider it a most just cause for war when a people which does not use its soil but keeps it idle and waste nevertheless forbids the use and possession of it to others who by the rule of nature ought to be maintained by it.

If ever any misfortune so diminishes the number in any of their cities that it cannot be made up out of

2. Resulting in approximately 156,000 adults for the whole state (city and country).

3. Under marriageable age, 22 for men, 18 for women.

other parts of the island without bringing other cities below their proper strength (this has happened, they say, only twice in all the ages on account of the raging of a fierce pestilence), they are filled up by citizens returning from colonial territory. They would rather that the colonies should perish than that any of the cities of the island should be enfeebled.

But to return to the dealings of the citizens. The oldest, as I have said, rules the household. Wives wait on their husbands, children on their parents, and generally the younger on their elders.

Every city is divided into four equal districts. In the middle of each quarter is a market of all kinds of commodities. To designated market buildings the products of each family are conveyed. Each kind of goods is arranged separately in storehouses. From the latter any head of a household seeks what he and his require and, without money or any kind of compensation, carries off what he seeks. Why should anything be refused? First, there is a plentiful supply of all things and, secondly, there is no underlying fear that anyone will demand more than he needs. Why should there be any suspicion that someone may demand an excessive amount when he is certain of never being in want? No doubt about it, avarice and greed are aroused in every kind of living creature by the fear of want, but only in man are they motivated by pride alone—pride which counts it a personal glory to excel others by superfluous display of possessions. The latter vice can have no place at all in the Utopian scheme of things.

Next to the market place that I have mentioned are the food markets. Here are brought not only different kinds of vegetables, fruit, and bread but also fish and whatever is edible of bird and four-footed beast. Outside the city are designated places where all gore and offal may be washed away in running water.[4] From these places they transport the carcasses of the animals slaughtered and cleaned by the hands of slaves. They do not allow their citizens to accustom themselves to the butchering of animals, by the practice of which they think that mercy, the finest feeling of our human nature, is gradually killed off. In addition, they do not permit to be brought inside the city anything filthy or unclean for fear that the air, tainted by putrefaction, should engender disease.

To continue, each street has spacious halls, located at equal distance from one another, each being known by a special name of its own. In these halls live the syphogrants. To each hall are assigned thirty families, fifteen on either side, to take their meals in common. The managers of each hall meet at a fixed time in the market and get food according to the number of persons in their individual charge.

Special care is first taken of the sick who are looked after in public hospitals. They have four at the city limits, a little outside the walls. These are so roomy as to be comparable to as many small towns. The purpose is twofold: first, that the sick, however numerous, should not be packed too close together in consequent discomfort and, second, that those who have a contagious disease likely to pass from one to another may be isolated as much as possible from the rest. These hospitals are very well furnished and equipped with everything conducive to health. Besides, such tender and careful treatment and such constant attendance of expert physicians are provided that, though no one is sent to them against his will, there is hardly anybody in the whole city who, when suffering from illness, does not prefer to be nursed there rather than at home.

4. Cf. "An Acte that noe Butcher slea any maner of beast within the Walles of London" (4° Hen. VII, 1488–89, c.3).

Book II

After the supervisor for the sick has received food as prescribed by the physicians, then the finest of everything is distributed equally among the halls according to the number in each, except that special regard is paid to the governor, the high priest, and the tranibors, as well as to ambassadors and all foreigners (if there are any, but they are few and far between). Yet the latter, too, when they are in Utopia, have definite homes got ready for them.

To these halls, at the hours fixed for dinner and supper, the entire syphograncy assembles, summoned by the blast of a brazen trumpet, excepting persons who are taking their meals either in the hospitals or at home. No one is forbidden, after the halls have been served, to fetch food from the market to his home: they realize that no one would do it without good reason. For, though nobody is forbidden to dine at home, yet no one does it willingly since the practice is considered not decent and since it is foolish to take the trouble of preparing an inferior dinner when an excellent and sumptuous one is ready at hand in the hall nearby.

In this hall all menial offices which to some degree involve heavy labor or soil the hands are performed by slaves. But the duty of cooking and preparing the food and, in fine, of arranging the whole meal is carried out by the women alone,[5] taking turns for each family. Persons sit down at three or more tables according to the number of the company. The men sit with their backs to the wall, the women on the outside, so that if they have any sudden pain or sickness, such as sometimes happens to women with child, they may rise without disturbing the arrangements and go to the nurses.

The nurses sit separately with the infants in a dining room assigned for the purpose, never without a fire and a supply of clean water nor without cradles. Thus they

5. Without crowds of servants.

can both lay the infants down and, when they wish, undo their wrappings and let them play freely by the fire. Each woman nurses her own offspring, unless prevented by either death or disease. When that happens, the wives of the syphogrants quickly provide a nurse and find no difficulty in doing so. The reason is that women who can do the service offer themselves with the greatest readiness since everybody praises this kind of pity and since the child who is thus fostered looks on his nurse as his natural mother. In the nurses' quarters are all children up to five years of age. All other minors, among whom they include all of both sexes below the age of marriage, either wait at table on the diners or, if they are not old and strong enough, stand by—and that in absolute silence. Both groups eat what is handed them from the table and have no other separate time for dining.

The syphogrant and his wife sit in the middle of the first table, which is the highest place and which allows them to have the whole company in view, for it stands crosswise at the farthest end of the dining room. Alongside them are two of the eldest, for they always sit four by four at all tables. But if there is a temple in the syphograncy, the priest and his wife so sit with the syphogrant as to preside. On both sides of them sit younger people, and next to them old people again, and so through the house those of the same age sit together and yet mingle with those of a different age. The reason for this practice, they say, is that the grave and reverend behavior of the old may restrain the younger people from mischievous freedom in word and gesture, since nothing can be done or said at table which escapes the notice of the old present on every side.

The trays of food are not served in order from the first place and so on, but all the old men, who are seated in conspicuous places, are served first with the best food, and then equal portions are given to the rest. The old men at their discretion give a share of their delicacies to their neighbors when there is not enough to go around to everybody in the house. Thus, due respect is paid to seniority, and yet all have an equal advantage.

They begin every dinner and supper with some reading which is conducive to morality but which is brief so as not to be tiresome.[6] Taking their cue from the reading, the elders introduce approved subjects of conversation, neither somber nor dull. But they do not monopolize the whole dinner with long speeches: they are ready to hear the young men too, and indeed deliberately draw them out that they may test each one's ability and character, which are revealed in the relaxed atmosphere of a feast.

Their dinners are somewhat short, their suppers more prolonged, because the former are followed by labor, the latter by sleep and a night's rest. They think the night's rest to be more efficacious to wholesome digestion. No supper passes without music, nor does the dessert course lack delicacies. They burn spices and scatter perfumes and omit nothing that may cheer the company. For they are somewhat more inclined to this attitude of mind: that no kind of pleasure is forbidden, provided no harm comes of it.

This is the common life they live in the city. In the country, however, since they are rather far removed from their neighbors, all take their meals in their own homes. No family lacks any kind of edible inasmuch as all the food eaten by the city dwellers comes from those who live in the country.

6. Such was More's custom (Stapleton, p. 97) and Colet's (Eras. *Ep.*, 4, 516). For its origin see Vergil, *Rer. invent.* 6.6, and for an example, Erasmus' colloquy "The Religious Banquet."

UTOPIAN TRAVEL, [ETC.]

Now if any citizens conceive a desire either to visit their friends who reside in another city or to see the place itself, they easily obtain leave from their syphogrants and tranibors, unless some good reason prevents them. Accordingly a party is made up and dispatched carrying a letter from the governor which bears witness to the granting of leave to travel and fixes the day of their return. A wagon is granted them with a public slave to conduct and see to the oxen, but, unless they have women in their company, they dispense with the wagon, regarding it as a burden and hindrance. Throughout their journey, though they carry nothing with them, yet nothing is lacking, for they are at home everywhere. If they stay longer than a day in any place, each practices his trade there and is entertained very courteously by workers in the same trade.

If any person gives himself leave to stray out of his territorial limits and is caught without the governor's certificate, he is treated with contempt, brought back as a runaway, and severely punished. If he dares to repeat the offense, he is punished with slavery.

If anyone is seized with the desire of exploring the country belonging to his own city, he is not forbidden to do so, provided he obtain his father's leave and his wife's consent. In any district of the country to which he comes, he receives no food until he has finished the morning share of the day's work or the labor that is usually performed there before supper. If he keep to this condition, he may go where he pleases within the territory belonging to his city. In this way he will be just as useful to the city as if he were in it.

Now you can see how nowhere is there any license to

waste time, nowhere any pretext to evade work—no wine shop, no alehouse, no brothel anywhere, no opportunity for corruption, no lurking hole, no secret meeting place. On the contrary, being under the eyes of all, people are bound either to be performing the usual labor or to be enjoying their leisure in a fashion not without decency. This universal behavior must of necessity lead to an abundance of all commodities. Since the latter are distributed evenly among all, it follows, of course, that no one can be reduced to poverty or beggary.

In the senate at Amaurotum (to which, as I said before, three are sent annually from every city), they first determine what commodity is in plenty in each particular place and again where on the island the crops have been meager. They at once fill up the scarcity of one place by the surplus of another. This service they perform without payment, receiving nothing in return from those to whom they give. Those who have given out of their stock to any particular city without requiring any return from it receive what they lack from another to which they have given nothing. Thus, the whole island is like a single family.[1]

But when they have made sufficient provision for themselves (which they do not consider complete until they have provided for two years to come, on account of the next year's uncertain crop), then they export into other countries, out of their surplus, a great quantity of grain, honey, wool, linen, timber, scarlet and purple dyestuffs, hides, wax, tallow, leather, as well as livestock. Of all these commodities they bestow the seventh part on the poor of the district and sell the rest at a moderate price.

By this trade they bring into their country not only such articles as they lack themselves—and practically the

1. "For what else is a kingdom but a great family?" (Erasmus, *Prince,* p. 170).

only thing lacking is iron[2]—but also a great quantity of silver and gold. This exchange has gone on day by day so long that now they have everywhere an abundance of these metals, more than would be believed. In consequence, they now care little whether they sell for ready cash or appoint a future day for payment, and in fact have by far the greatest amount out on credit. In all transactions on credit, however, they never trust private citizens but the municipal government, the legal documents being drawn up as usual. When the day for payment comes, the city collects the money due from private debtors and puts it into the treasury and enjoys the use of it until the Utopians claim payment.

The Utopians never claim payment of most of the money. They think it hardly fair to take away a thing useful to other people when it is useless to themselves. But if circumstances require that they should lend some part of it to another nation, then they call in their debts —or when they must wage war. It is for that single purpose that they keep all the treasure they possess at home: to be their bulwark in extreme peril or in sudden emergency. They use it above all to hire at sky-high rates of pay foreign mercenaries (whom they would jeopardize rather than their own citizens), being well aware that by large sums of money even their enemies themselves may be bought and set to fight one another either by treachery or by open warfare.

For these military reasons they keep a vast treasure, but not as a treasure. They keep it in a way which I am really quite ashamed to reveal for fear that my words will not be believed. My fears are all the more justified because I am conscious that, had I not been there and witnessed the phenomenon, I myself should have been

2. On "large imports from abroad" after 1450 see H. R. Schubert, *History of the British Iron and Steel Industry* (London, 1957), p. 145.

with difficulty induced to believe it from another's account. It needs must be almost always the rule that, as far as a thing is unlike the ways of the hearers, so far is it from obtaining their credence. An impartial judge of things, however, seeing that the rest of their institutions are so unlike ours, will perhaps wonder less that their use of silver and gold should be adapted to their way of life rather than to ours. As stated, they do not use money themselves but keep it only for an emergency, which may actually occur, yet possibly may never happen.

Meanwhile, gold and silver, of which money is made, are so treated by them that no one values them more highly than their true nature deserves. Who does not see that they are far inferior to iron in usefulness since without iron mortals cannot live any more than without fire and water? To gold and silver, however, nature has given no use that we cannot dispense with, if the folly of men had not made them valuable because they are rare. On the other hand, like a most kind and indulgent mother, she has exposed to view all that is best, like air and water and earth itself, but has removed as far as possible from us all vain and unprofitable things.

If in Utopia these metals were kept locked up in a tower, it might be suspected that the governor and the senate—for such is the foolish imagination of the common folk—were deceiving the people by the scheme and they themselves were deriving some benefit therefrom. Moreover, if they made them into drinking vessels and other such skillful handiwork, then if occasion arose for them all to be melted down again and applied to the pay of soldiers, they realize that people would be unwilling to be deprived of what they had once begun to treasure.

To avoid these dangers, they have devised a means which, as it is consonant with the rest of their institutions, so it is extremely unlike our own—seeing that we

value gold so much and are so careful in safeguarding it
—and therefore incredible except to those who have
experience of it. While they eat and drink from earthen-
ware and glassware of fine workmanship but of little
value, from gold and silver they make chamber pots and
all the humblest vessels for use everywhere, not only in
the common halls but in private homes also. Moreover,
they employ the same metals to make the chains and
solid fetters which they put on their slaves. Finally, as
for those who bear the stigma of disgrace on account of
some crime, they have gold ornaments hanging from
their ears, gold rings encircling their fingers, gold chains
thrown around their necks, and, as a last touch, a gold
crown binding their temples. Thus by every means in
their power they make gold and silver a mark of ill
fame. In this way, too, it happens that, while all other
nations bear the loss of these metals with as great grief
as if they were losing their very vitals, if circumstances
in Utopia ever required the removal of all gold and
silver, no one would feel that he were losing as much as
a penny.

They also gather pearls by the seashore and diamonds
and rubies on certain cliffs. They do not look for them
purposely, but they polish them when found by chance.
With them they adorn little children, who in their earliest years are proud and delighted with such decorations.
When they have grown somewhat older and perceive
that only children use such toys, they lay them aside, not
by any order of their parents, but through their own feeling of shame, just as our own children, when they grow
up, throw away their marbles, rattles, and dolls.

What opposite ideas and feelings are created by customs so different from those of other people came home
to me never more clearly than in the case of the Anemolian[3] ambassadors. They arrived in Amaurotum dur-

3. 'Windy People,' i.e. 'Vain, Conceited, Inconstant People.'

ing my stay there. Because they came to treat of important matters, the three representatives of each city had assembled before their appearance. Now all the ambassadors of neighboring nations, who had previously visited the land, were well acquainted with the manners of the Utopians and knew that they paid no respect to costly clothes but looked with contempt on silk and regarded gold as a badge of disgrace. These persons usually came in the simplest possible dress. But the Anemolians, living farther off and having had fewer dealings with them, since they heard that in Utopia all were dressed alike, and in a homespun fashion at that, felt sure that they did not possess what they made no use of. Being more proud than wise, they determined by the grandeur of their apparel to represent the gods themselves and by their splendid adornment to dazzle the eyes of the poor Utopians.

Consequently the three ambassadors made a grand entry with a suite of a hundred followers, all in particolored clothes and most in silk. The ambassadors themselves, being noblemen at home, were arrayed in cloth of gold, with heavy gold necklaces and earrings, with gold rings on their fingers, and with strings of gleaming pearls and gems upon their caps; in fact, they were decked out with all those articles which in Utopia are used to punish slaves, to stigmatize evil-doers, or to amuse children. It was a sight worth seeing to behold their cockiness when they compared their grand clothing with that of the Utopians, who had poured out into the street to see them pass. On the other hand, it was no less delightful to notice how much they were mistaken in their sanguine expectations and how far they were from obtaining the consideration which they had hoped to get. To the eyes of all the Utopians, with the exception of the very few who for a good reason had visited foreign countries, all this gay show appeared disgraceful. They therefore bowed to the lowest of the party as to the masters but took the ambassadors themselves to be slaves because they were wearing gold chains, and passed them over without any deference whatever.

Why, you might have seen also the children who had themselves discarded gems and pearls, when they saw them attached to the caps of the ambassadors, poke and nudge their mothers and say to them:

"Look, mother, that big rascal is still wearing pearls and jewels as if he were yet a little boy!"

But the mother, also in earnest, would say:

"Hush, son, I think it is one of the ambassadors' fools."

Others found fault with the golden chains as useless, being so slender that a slave could easily break them or, again, so loose that at his pleasure he could throw them off and escape anywhere scot-free.

After spending one or more days there, the ambassadors saw an immense quantity of gold held as cheaply and in as great contempt there as in honor among themselves. They saw, too, that more gold and silver were amassed to make the chains and fetters of one runaway slave than had made up the whole array of the three of them. They then were crestfallen and for shame put away all the finery with which they had made themselves haughtily conspicuous, especially when, after familiar talk with the Utopians, they had learned their ways and opinions.

The Utopians wonder that any mortal takes pleasure in the uncertain sparkle of a tiny jewel or precious stone when he can look at a star or even the sun itself. They wonder that anyone can be so mad as to think himself more noble on account of the texture of a finer wool, since, however fine the texture is, a sheep once wore the wool and yet all the time was nothing more than a sheep.

Book II

They wonder, too, that gold, which by its very nature is so useless, is now everywhere in the world valued so highly that man himself, through whose agency and for whose use it got this value, is priced much cheaper than gold itself. This is true to such an extent that a blockhead[4] who has no more intelligence than a log and who is as dishonest as he is foolish keeps in bondage many wise men and good men merely for the reason that a great heap of gold coins happens to be his. Yet if some chance or some legal trick (which is as apt as chance to confound high and low) transfers it from this master to the lowest rascal in his entire household, he will surely very soon pass into the service of his former servant—as if he were a mere appendage of and addition to the coins! But much more do they wonder at and abominate the madness of persons who pay almost divine honors to the rich, to whom they neither owe anything nor are obligated in any other respect than that they are rich. Yet they know them to be so mean and miserly that they are more than sure that of all that great pile of cash, as long as the rich men live, not a single penny will ever come their way.

These and similar opinions they have conceived partly from their upbringing, being reared in a commonwealth whose institutions are far removed from follies of the kind mentioned, and partly from instruction and reading good books. Though there are not many in each city who are relieved from all other tasks and assigned to scholarship alone, that is to say, the individuals in whom they have detected from childhood an outstanding personality, a first-rate intelligence, and an inclination of mind toward learning, yet all children are introduced to good literature. A large part of the people, too, men and women alike, throughout their lives, devote to learn-

4. Lit. 'leaden, leaden-witted,' perhaps in contrast with gold.

ing the hours which, as we said, are free from manual labor.[5]

They learn the various branches of knowledge in their native tongue. The latter is copious in vocabulary and pleasant to the ear and a very faithful exponent of thought. It is almost the same as that current in a great part of that side of the world, only that everywhere else its form is more corrupt, to different degrees in different regions.

Of all those philosophers whose names are famous in the part of the world known to us, the reputation of not even a single one had reached them before our arrival. Yet in music, dialectic,[6] arithmetic, and geometry they have made almost the same discoveries as those predecessors of ours in the classical world. But while they measure up to the ancients in almost all other subjects, still they are far from being a match for the inventions of our modern logicians.[7] In fact, they have discovered not even a single one of those very ingeniously devised rules about restrictions, amplifications, and suppositions which our own children everywhere learn in the *Small Logicals*.[8] In addition, so far are they from ability to speculate on second intentions[9] that not one of them could

5. On resistance of the English gentry and nobility to learning, see More, *Corresp.*, pp. 403–05; Elyot, *Gou.* 1.12; Pace, *Fruct.*, p. 15; and Dudley, *The Tree of Commonwealth*, ed. D. M. Brodie (Cambridge, 1948), p. 45.

6. To be studied as a tool, not an end in itself, according to the humanists.

7. The Schoolmen.

8. Authored by Peter of Spain; see More's *S.L.*, p. 20.

9. Whereas the first intention is the direct apprehension of a thing according to its nature, the second is the form resulting from the intellect's triple reflection: upon itself, upon its way of apprehension, and upon the manner in which the nature of a thing exists in the intellect. It exists only in the intellect and therefore is "no where" (More, *Works*, p. 748).

Book II

see even man himself as a so-called universal[10]—though he was, as you know, colossal and greater than any giant, as well as pointed out by us with our finger.

They are most expert, however, in the courses of the stars and the movements of the celestial bodies. Moreover, they have ingeniously devised instruments in different shapes, by which they have most exactly comprehended the movements and positions of the sun and moon and all the other stars which are visible in their horizon. But of the agreements and discords of the planets and, in sum, of all that infamous and deceitful divination by the stars, they do not even dream.

They forecast rains, winds, and all the other changes in weather by definite signs which they have ascertained by long practice. But as to the *causes* of all these phenomena, and of the flow of the sea and its saltiness, and, in fine, of the origin and nature of the heavens and the universe, they partly treat of them in the same way as our ancient philosophers and partly, as the latter differ from one another, they, too, in introducing new theories disagree with them all and yet do not in all respects agree with fellow Utopians.

In that part of philosophy which deals with morals, they carry on the same debates as we do. They inquire into the good: of the soul and of the body and of external gifts. They ask also whether the name of good may be applied to all three or simply belongs to the endowments of the soul. They discuss virtue and pleasure, but their principal and chief debate is in what thing or things, one or more, they are to hold that happiness consists. In this matter they seem to lean more than they should to the school that espouses pleasure as the object by which to define either the whole or the chief part of human happiness.

10. A nature perceived as predicable of many inferiors or individuals. For a similar gibe see Erasmus, *Folly*, pp. 77, 79.

What is more astonishing is that they seek a defense for this soft doctrine from their religion, which is serious and strict, almost solemn and hard. They never have a discussion of happiness without uniting certain principles taken from religion as well as from philosophy, which uses rational arguments. Without these principles they think reason insufficient and weak by itself for the investigation of true happiness. The following are examples of these principles. The soul is immortal and by the goodness of God born for happiness. After this life rewards are appointed for our virtues and good deeds, punishment for our crimes. Though these principles belong to religion, yet they hold that reason leads men to believe and to admit them.[11]

Once the principles are eliminated, the Utopians have no hesitation in maintaining that a person would be stupid not to realize that he ought to seek pleasure by fair means or foul, but that he should only take care not to let a lesser pleasure interfere with a greater nor to follow after a pleasure which would bring pain in retaliation. To pursue hard and painful virtue and not only to banish the sweetness of life but even voluntarily to suffer pain from which you expect no profit (for what profit can there be if after death you gain nothing for having passed the whole present life unpleasantly, that is, wretchedly?)—this policy they declare to be the extreme of madness.

As it is, they hold happiness rests not in every kind of pleasure but only in good and decent pleasure.[12] To such, as to the supreme good, our nature is drawn by virtue itself, to which the opposite school alone attributes happiness. The Utopians define virtue as living accord-

11. Reason and faith are always allies (More, *S.L.*, p. 237; *Works*, pp. 257, 368).

12. Epicurus' pleasure is really "sober and abstemious" (Sen. *Vit. Beat.* 7.12.4); pleasure should be "attended by honour" (Isoc. *Or.* 1.16, 1.46).

ing to nature since to this end we were created by God. That individual, they say, is following the guidance of nature who, in desiring one thing and avoiding another, obeys the dictates of reason.

Now reason first of all inflames men to a love and veneration of the divine majesty, to whom we owe both our existence and our capacity for happiness. Secondly, it admonishes and urges us to lead a life as free from care and as full of joy as possible and, because of our natural fellowship, to help all other men, too, to attain that end. No one was ever so solemn and severe a follower of virtue and hater of pleasure that he, while imposing on you labors, watchings, and discomforts, would not at the same time bid you do your best to relieve the poverty and misfortunes of others. He would bid you regard as praiseworthy in humanity's name that one man should provide for another man's welfare and comfort— if it is especially humane (and humanity is the virtue most peculiar to man) to relieve the misery of others and, by taking away all sadness from their life, restore them to enjoyment, that is, to pleasure. If so, why should not nature urge everyone to do the same for himself also?

For either a joyous life, that is, a pleasurable life, is evil, in which case not only ought you to help no one to it but, as far as you can, should take it away from everyone as being harmful and deadly, or else, if you not only are permitted but are obliged to win it for others as being good, why should you not do so first of all for yourself, to whom you should show no less favor than to others? When nature bids you to be good to others, she does not command you conversely to be cruel and merciless to yourself. So nature herself, they maintain, prescribes to us a joyous life or, in other words, pleasure, as the end of all our operations. Living according to her prescription they define as virtue.

To pursue this line. Nature calls all men to help one

another to a merrier life. (This she certainly does with good reason, for no one is raised so far above the common lot of mankind as to have his sole person the object of nature's care, seeing that she equally favors all whom she endows with the same form.) Consequently nature surely bids you take constant care not so to further your own advantages as to cause disadvantages to your fellows.

Therefore they hold that not only ought contracts between private persons to be observed but also public laws for the distribution of vital commodities, that is to say, the matter of pleasure,[13] provided they have been justly promulgated by a good king[14] or ratified by the common consent of a people neither oppressed by tyranny nor deceived by fraud. As long as such laws are not broken, it is prudence to look after your own interests, and to look after those of the public in addition is a mark of devotion. But to deprive others of their pleasure to secure your own, this is surely an injustice. On the contrary, to take away something from yourself and to give it to others is a duty of humanity and kindness which never takes away as much advantage as it brings back. It is compensated by the return of benefits as well as by the actual consciousness of the good deed. Remembrance of the love and good will of those whom you have benefited gives the mind a greater amount of pleasure than the bodily pleasure which you have forgone would have afforded. Finally—and religion easily brings this home to a mind which readily assents—God repays, in place of a brief and tiny pleasure, immense and neverending gladness.[15] And so they maintain, having carefully considered and weighed the matter, that all our actions,

13. *Matter* is an Aristotelico-Scholastic term for the undetermined but determinable element of pleasure (food, clothing, housing, etc.), as opposed to the *form* (either private ownership or communism).

14. Like Utopus.

15. *Gaudium,* a theological term for joy of beatific vision.

and even the very virtues exercised in them, look at last to pleasure as their end and happiness.[16]

By pleasure they understand every movement and state of body or mind in which, under the guidance of nature, man delights to dwell. They are right in including man's natural inclinations. For just as the senses as well as right reason aim at whatever is pleasant by nature—whatever is not striven after through wrong-doing, nor involves the loss of something more pleasant, nor is followed by pain[17]—so they hold that whatever things mortals imagine by a futile consensus to be sweet to them in spite of being against nature (as though they had the power to change the nature of things as they do their names) are all so far from making for happiness that they are even a great hindrance to it. The reason is that they possess the minds of persons in whom they have once become deep-seated with a false idea of pleasure so that no room is left anywhere for true and genuine delights. In fact, very many are the things which, though of their own nature they contain no sweetness, nay, a good part of them very much bitterness, still are, through the perverse attraction of evil desires, not only regarded as the highest pleasures but also counted among the chief reasons that make life worth living.

In the class that follow this spurious pleasure, they put those whom I mentioned before, who think themselves the better men, the better the coat they wear. In this one thing they make a twofold mistake: they are no less deceived in thinking their coat better than in thinking themselves better. If you consider the use of the garment, why is wool of finer thread superior to that of thicker? Yet, as if it were by nature and not by their own mistake that they had the advantage, they hold their heads high and believe some extra worth attaches to

16. Cf. Cic. *Fin.* 1.16.54, *Off.* 3.33.116–18.
17. The most explicit statement of the criteria for true pleasure.

themselves thereby. Thus, the honor which, if ill-clad, they would not have ventured to hope for, they require as if of right for a smarter coat. If passed by with some neglect, they are indignant.

Again, does it not show the same stupidity to think so much of empty and unprofitable honors? [18] What natural and true pleasure can another's bared head or bent knees afford you? Will this behavior cure the pain in your own knees or relieve the lunacy in your own head? In this conception of counterfeit pleasure, a strange and sweet madness is displayed by men who imagine themselves to be noble and plume themselves on it and applaud themselves because their fortune has been to be born of certain ancestors of whom the long succession has been counted rich—for that is now the only nobility —and especially rich in landed estates.[19] They consider themselves not a whit less noble even if their ancestors have not left them a square foot or if they themselves have consumed in extravagant living what was left them.

With these persons they class those who, as I said, dote on jewels and gems and who think they become a species of god if ever they secure a fine specimen, especially of the sort which at the period is regarded as of the highest value in their country. It is not everywhere or always that one kind of stone is prized. They will not purchase it unless taken out of its gold setting and exposed to view, and not even then unless the seller takes an oath and gives security that it is a true gem and a true stone, so anxious are they lest a spurious stone in place of a genuine one deceive their eyes. But why should a counterfeited one give less pleasure to your sight when your eye cannot distinguish it from the true article? Both

18. "True honor is that which follows on virtue and right action of its own will" (Erasmus, *Prince*, p. 148).

19. Especially characteristic of the English, according to Poggio ("De nobilitate," *Opera* [Strasbourg, 1513], fol.26ᵛ).

should be of equal value to you, even as they would be, by heaven, to a blind man!

What can be said of those who keep superfluous wealth to please themselves, not with putting the heap to any use but merely with looking at it?[20] Do they feel true pleasure, or are they not rather cheated by false pleasure? Or, what of those who have the opposite failing and hide the gold, which they will never use and perhaps never see again, and who, in their anxiety not to lose it, thereby do lose it? What else but loss is it to deprive yourself of its use, and perhaps all other men too, and to put it back in the ground? And yet you joyfully exult over your hidden treasure as though your mind were now free from all anxiety. Suppose that someone removed it by stealing it and that you died ten years afterwards knowing nothing of the theft. During the whole decade which you lived after the money was stolen, what did it matter to you whether it was stolen or safe? In either case it was of just as little use to you.

Among those who indulge such senseless delights they reckon dicers (whose madness they know not by experience but by hearsay only), as well as hunters and hawkers. What pleasure is there, they ask, in shooting dice upon a table? You have shot them so often that, even if some pleasure had been in it, weariness by now could have arisen from the habitual practice. Or what sweetness can there be, and not rather disgust, in hearing the barking and howling of dogs? Or what greater sensation of pleasure is there when a dog chases a hare than when a dog chases a dog? The same thing happens in both cases: there is racing in both if speed gives you delight.

But if you are attracted by the hope of slaughter and the expectation of a creature being mangled under your eyes, it ought rather to inspire pity when you behold a

20. Money is for *use*. Cf. More, *Epigr.*, p. 179, and Pl. *Rep.* 8.554 A–B, *Leg.* 5.743 A–C, 8.831 C.

weak, fugitive, timid, and innocent little hare torn to pieces by a strong, fierce, and cruel dog. In consequence the Utopians have imposed the whole activity of hunting, as unworthy of free men, upon their butchers—a craft, as I explained before, they exercise through their slaves. They regard hunting as the meanest part of the butcher's trade and its other functions as more useful and more honorable, seeing that they do much more positive good and kill animals only from necessity, whereas the hunter seeks nothing but pleasure from the killing and mangling of a poor animal. Even in the case of brute beasts, this desire of looking on bloodshed, in their estimation, either arises from a cruel disposition or degenerates finally into cruelty through the constant practice of such brutal pleasure.

Although the mob of mortals regards these and all similar pursuits—and they are countless—as pleasures, yet the Utopians positively hold them to have nothing to do with true pleasure since there is nothing sweet in them by nature. The fact that for the mob they inspire in the senses a feeling of enjoyment—which seems to be the function of pleasure—does not make them alter their opinion. The enjoyment does not arise from the nature of the thing itself but from their own perverse habit. The latter failing makes them take what is bitter for sweet, just as pregnant women by their vitiated taste suppose pitch and tallow sweeter than honey. Yet it is impossible for any man's judgment, depraved either by disease or by habit, to change the nature of pleasure any more than that of anything else.

The pleasures which they admit as genuine they divide into various classes, some pleasures being attributed to the soul and others to the body. To the soul they ascribe intelligence and the sweetness which is bred of contemplation of truth. To these two are joined the pleasant recollection of a well-spent life and the sure hope of happiness to come.

Bodily pleasure they divide into two kinds. The first is that which fills the sense with clearly perceptible sweetness. Sometimes it comes from the renewal of those organs which have been weakened by our natural heat. These organs are then restored by food and drink. Sometimes it comes from the elimination of things which overload the body. This agreeable sensation occurs when we discharge feces from our bowels or perform the activity generative of children or relieve the itching of some part by rubbing or scratching. Now and then, however, pleasure arises, not in process of restoring anything that our members lack, nor in process of eliminating anything that causes distress, but from something that tickles and affects our senses with a secret but remarkable moving force and so draws them to itself. Such is that pleasure which is engendered by music.

The second kind of bodily pleasure they claim to be that which consists in a calm and harmonious state of the body. This is nothing else than each man's health undisturbed by any disorder. Health, if assailed by no pain, gives delight of itself, though there be no motion arising from pleasure applied from without. Even though it is less obvious and less perceptible by the sense than that overblown craving for eating and drinking, yet none the less many hold it to be the greatest of pleasures. Almost all the Utopians regard it as great and as practically the foundation and basis of all pleasures. Even by itself it can make the state of life peaceful and desirable, whereas without it absolutely no place is left for any pleasure. The absence of pain without the presence of health they regard as insensibility rather than pleasure.

They long ago rejected the position of those who held that a state of stable and tranquil health (for this question, too, had been actively discussed among them) was not to be counted as a pleasure because its presence, they said, could not be felt except through some motion from without. But on the other hand now they almost all agree that health is above all things conducive to pleasure. Since in disease, they query, there is pain, which is the bitter enemy of pleasure no less than disease is of health, why should not pleasure in turn be found in the tranquillity of health? They think that it is of no importance in the discussion whether you say that disease is pain or that disease is accompanied with pain, for it comes to the same thing either way. To be sure, if you hold that health is either a pleasure or the necessary cause of pleasure, as fire is of heat, in both ways the conclusion is that those who have permanent health cannot be without pleasure.

Besides, while we eat, say they, what is that but health, which has begun to be impaired, fighting against hunger, with food as its comrade in arms? While it gradually gains strength, the very progress to the usual vigor supplies the pleasure by which we are thus restored. Shall the health which delights in conflict not rejoice when it has gained the victory? When at length it has successfully acquired its former strength, which was its sole object through the conflict, shall it immediately become insensible and not recognize and embrace its own good? The assertion that health cannot be felt they think to be far wide of the truth. Who in a waking state, ask they, does not feel that he is in good health—except the man who is not? Who is bound fast by such insensibility or lethargy that he does not confess that health is agreeable and delightful to him? And what is delight except pleasure under another name?

To sum up, they cling above all to mental pleasures, which they value as the first and foremost of all pleasures. Of these the principal part they hold to arise from the practice of the virtues and the consciousness of a good life. Of those pleasures which the body supplies, they give the palm to health. The delight of eating and drinking, and anything that gives the same sort of enjoyment, they think desirable, but only for the sake of health. Such things are not pleasant in themselves but only in so far as they resist the secret encroachment of ill health. Just as a wise man should pray that he may escape disease rather than crave a remedy for it and that he may drive pain off rather than seek relief from it, so it would be better not to need this kind of pleasure rather than to be soothed by it.

If a person thinks that his felicity consists in this kind of pleasure, he must admit that he will be in the greatest happiness if his lot happens to be a life which is spent in perpetual hunger, thirst, itching, eating, drinking, scratching, and rubbing. Who does not see that such a life is not only disgusting but wretched? These pleasures are surely the lowest of all as being most adulterated, for they never occur unless they are coupled with the pains which are their opposites. For example, with the pleasure of eating is united hunger—and on no fair terms, for the pain is the stronger and lasts the longer. It comes into existence before the pleasure and does not end until the pleasure dies with it. Such pleasures they hold should not be highly valued and only insofar as they are necessary. Yet they enjoy even these pleasures and gratefully acknowledge the kindness of mother nature who, with alluring sweetness, coaxes her offspring to that which of necessity they must constantly do. In what discomfort should we have to live if, like all other sicknesses which less frequently assail us, so also these daily diseases of hunger and thirst had to be expelled by bitter poisons and drugs?

Beauty, strength, and nimbleness—these as special and pleasant gifts of nature they gladly cherish. Nay, even those pleasures entering by the ears, eyes, or nostrils, which nature intended to be peculiarly characteristic of man (for no other species of living creature either takes in the form and fairness of the world or is affected by the pleasantness of smell, except in choice of food, or distinguishes harmonious and dissonant intervals of sound) —these, too, I say, they follow after as pleasant seasonings of life. But in all they make this limitation: that the lesser is not to interfere with the greater and that pleasure is not to produce pain in aftermath. Pain they think a necessary consequence if the pleasure is base.

But to despise the beauty of form, to impair the strength of the body, to turn nimbleness into sluggishness, to exhaust the body by fasts, to injure one's health, and to reject all the other favors of nature, unless a man neglects these advantages to himself in providing more zealously for the pleasure of other persons or of the public, in return for which sacrifice he expects a greater pleasure from God—but otherwise to deal harshly with oneself for a vain and shadowy reputation of virtue to no man's profit or for preparing oneself more easily to bear adversities which may never come—this attitude they think is extreme madness and the sign of a mind which is both cruel to itself and ungrateful to nature, to whom it disdains to be indebted and therefore renounces all her benefits.

This is their view of virtue and pleasure. They believe that human reason can attain to no truer view, unless a heaven-sent religion inspire man with something more holy.[21] Whether in this stand they are right or wrong, time does not permit us to examine—nor is it necessary. We have taken upon ourselves only to describe their principles, and not also to defend them. But of this I am sure, that whatever you think of their ideas, there is nowhere in the world a more excellent people nor a happier commonwealth. They are nimble and active of

21. Reason must yield before faith (cf. More, *Works,* p. 839).

Book II

body, and stronger than you would expect from their stature. The latter, however, is not dwarfish. Though they have not a very fertile soil or a very wholesome climate,[22] they protect themselves against the atmosphere by temperate living and make up for the defects of the land by diligent labor. Consequently, nowhere in the world is there a more plentiful supply of grain and cattle, nowhere are men's bodies more vigorous and subject to fewer diseases. Not only may you behold the usual agricultural tasks carefully administered there, whereby the naturally barren soil is improved by art and industry, but you may also see how a whole forest has been uprooted in one place by the hands of the people and planted in another. Herein they were thinking not so much of abundance as of transport, that they might have wood closer to the sea or the rivers or the cities themselves. For it takes less labor to convey grain than timber to a distance by land.

The people in general are easygoing, good-tempered, ingenious, and leisure-loving. They patiently do their share of manual labor when occasion demands, though otherwise they are by no means fond of it. In their devotion to mental study they are unwearied. When they had heard from us about the literature and learning of the Greeks[23] (for in Latin there was nothing, apart from history and poetry, which seemed likely to gain their great approval), it was wonderful to see their extreme desire for permission to master them through our instruction.

We began, therefore, to give them public lessons, more at first that we should not seem to refuse the trouble

22. Britain is inferior to France but superior to Ireland, according to *Saint Albans Chronicle*, sig. A₂.

23. Hythlodaeus, as has already been mentioned, is expert in Greek. Cf. More, *S.L.*, pp. 50–54, 94–103. More approved the simultaneous study of Greek and Latin (*Corresp.*, p. 403).

than that we expected any success. But after a little progress, their diligence made us at once feel sure that our own diligence would not be bestowed in vain. They began so easily to imitate the shapes of the letters, so readily to pronounce the words, so quickly to learn by heart, and so faithfully to reproduce what they had learned that it was a perfect wonder to us. The explanation was that most of them were scholars picked for their ability and mature in years, who undertook to learn their tasks not only fired by their own free will but acting under orders of the senate. In less than three years they were perfect in the language and able to peruse good authors without any difficulty unless the text had faulty readings.[24] According to my conjecture, they got hold of Greek literature more easily because it was somewhat related to their own. I suspect that their race was derived from the Greek because their language, which in almost all other respects resembles the Persian, retains some traces of Greek in the names of their cities and officials.

When about to go on the fourth voyage, I put on board, in place of wares to sell, a fairly large package of books, having made up my mind never to return rather than to come back soon. They received from me most of Plato's[25] works, several of Aristotle's, as well as Theophrastus[26] on plants, which I regret to say was mutilated in parts. During the voyage an ape found the book, left lying carelessly about, and in wanton sport tore out and destroyed several pages in various sections. Of grammarians they have only Lascaris, for I did not take

24. Preparation of correct texts was a major task of the humanists.

25. The author with greatest influence on *Utopia* comes first. For More's predilection, see Stapleton, p. 15.

26. The pupil and successor of Aristotle, whose works on plants later became less popular than his *Characters*.

Book II

Theodore[27] with me. They have no dictionaries except those of Hesychius and Dioscorides.[28] They are very fond of the works of Plutarch[29] and captivated by the wit and pleasantry of Lucian.[30] Of the poets they have Aristophanes, Homer, and Euripides, together with Sophocles in the small Aldine type.[31] Of the historians they possess Thucydides and Herodotus, as well as Herodian.[32]

In medicine, moreover, my companion Tricius Apinatus[33] had carried with him some small treatises of Hippocrates and the *Ars medica* of Galen,[34] to which books they attribute great value. Even though there is scarcely a nation in the whole world that needs medicine less,[35] yet nowhere is it held in greater honor—and this for the reason that they regard the knowledge of it as

27. In general, Theodore of Gaza (d. 1475) was preferred to Constantine Lascaris (d. 1501). Cf. Erasmus, *Opera, I*, 521.

28. Hesychius was first published in Venice in 1514. Dioscorides' *Materia medica,* in a Latin translation by Jehan Ruelle, appeared in 1516.

29. Several of his works were translated into Latin by Erasmus.

30. A number of Lucian's writings were published in Latin translations by More and Erasmus in 1506.

31. Hythlodaeus is more liberal than Socrates (*Rep.* 10.607A; cf. *Leg.* 7.801D–02D). For More's defense of poetry see *Works*, p. 153. Aldus Manutius died on February 6, 1515.

32. Herodian of Antioch's history of the Roman emperors from 180 to 238 had been translated by Poliziano. There is a modern English version by E. C. Echols (Berkeley, 1961).

33. The name is of course fictitious. Apina and Trica, little towns in Apulia, were so ignominiously overwhelmed by Diomedes that they became a symbol of ridiculous trifles (Mart. 14.1.7, Plin. *HN* 3.11[16], Eras. *Adag.* 143).

34. Called *Ars parva* or *Microtechne* in the Middle Ages, an extremely popular compendium of his medical notions. Linacre's Latin translation of Galen's *Preservation of Health* appeared in 1517. Cf. More, *S.L.*, p. 87.

35. On the need of physicians as a symptom of degeneracy see Pl. *Rep.* 3.405A–08E.

one of the finest and most useful branches of philosophy. When by the help of this philosophy they explore the secrets of nature,[36] they appear to themselves not only to get great pleasure in doing so but also to win the highest approbation of the Author and Maker of nature.[37] They presume that, like all other artificers, He has set forth the visible mechanism of the world as a spectacle for man, whom alone He has made capable of appreciating such a wonderful thing. Therefore He prefers a careful and diligent beholder and admirer of His work to one who like an unreasoning brute beast passes by so great and so wonderful a spectacle stupidly and stolidly.

Thus, trained in all learning, the minds of the Utopians are exceedingly apt in the invention of the arts which promote the advantage and convenience of life. Two, however, they owe to us, the art of printing and the manufacture of paper[38]—though not entirely to us but to a great extent also to themselves. When we showed them the Aldine printing in paper books, we talked about the material of which paper is made and the art of printing without giving a detailed explanation, for none of us was expert in either art. With the greatest acuteness they promptly guessed how it was done. Though previously they wrote only on parchment, bark, and papyrus, from this time they tried to manufacture paper and print letters. Their first attempts were not very successful, but by frequent experiment they soon mastered both. So great was their success that if they had copies of Greek authors, they would have no lack of books. But

36. More speaks elsewhere of philosophers' pleasure in beholding "the secret draughts of nature" (*Works*, prelim. sig. ([₇v); cf. also *S.L.*, p. 52.

37. Cf. Cic. *Nat. D.* 2.29.73–2.67.168 on the world's witness to divine existence, creation, and providence.

38. The process reached France by the twelfth century via the Chinese, Arabs, and Spanish.

at present they have no more than I have mentioned, but by printing books they have increased their stock by many thousands of copies.

Whoever, coming to their land on a sight-seeing tour, is recommended by any special intellectual endowment or is acquainted with many countries through long travel, is sure of a hearty welcome, for they delight in hearing what is happening in the whole world. On this score our own landing was pleasing to them. Few persons, however, come to them in the way of trade. What could they bring except iron, or what everybody would rather take back home with him—gold and silver! And as to articles of export, the Utopians think it wiser to carry them out of the country themselves than to let strangers come to fetch them. By this policy they get more information about foreign nations and do not forget by disuse their skill in navigation.[39]

SLAVERY, [ETC.]

Prisoners of war are not enslaved unless captured in wars fought by the Utopians themselves; nor are the sons of slaves, nor anyone who was in slavery when acquired of slaves, nor anyone whom they could acquire from slavery in other countries. Their slaves[1] are either such or such as have been condemned to death elsewhere for some offense. The greater number are of this latter kind. They carry away many of them; sometimes they buy

39. On its necessity cf. Arist. *Pol.* 7.5.6, 1327a–b. On English concern see 1° Hen. VII, 1485, c.8; 4° Hen. VII, 1488–89, c.10; and Starkey, *Dialogue*, p. 174.

1. The ambiguous Latin term *seruus* can mean 'subject,' 'vassal,' 'servant,' 'serf,' or 'slave' in the strict sense. Like Duns Scotus (*Op. Ox.*, 4, d. 36, q. 1, n. 2), the Utopians recognize three titles: capture in war, punishment for crime, and voluntary enslavement. There was a resurgence of slavery through contemporary contact with negroes in Africa and with Indians in America.

them cheaply; but often they ask for them and get them for nothing. These classes of slaves they keep not only continually at work but also in chains. Their own countrymen are dealt with more harshly, since their conduct is regarded as all the more regrettable and deserving a more severe punishment as an object lesson because, having had an excellent rearing to a virtuous life, they still could not be restrained from crime.

There is yet another class of slaves, for sometimes a hard-working and poverty-stricken drudge of another country voluntarily chooses slavery in Utopia. These individuals are well treated and, except that they have a little more work assigned to them as being used to it, are dealt with almost as leniently as citizens. If anyone wishes to depart, which seldom happens, they do not detain him against his will nor send him away emptyhanded.

The sick, as I said, are very lovingly cared for, nothing being omitted which may restore them to health, whether in the way of medicine or diet. They console the incurably diseased by sitting and conversing with them and by applying all possible alleviations. But if a disease is not only incurable but also distressing and agonizing without any cessation, then the priests and the public officials exhort the man, since he is now unequal to all life's duties, a burden to himself, and a trouble to others, and is living beyond the time of his death, to make up his mind not to foster the pest and plague any longer nor to hesitate to die now that life is torture to him but, relying on good hope, to free himself from this bitter life as from prison and the rack, or else voluntarily to permit others to free him.[2] In this course he will act

2. On suicide see More, *Works*, pp. 1188–98. Traditional Christian teaching is found in Aug. *De Civ. D.* 1.17–27, and Aquinas, *S.T.* 2–2, q. 64, a.5. For ancient views see Pl. *Leg.* 9.873C; Diog. Laert. 7.130, 10.119; Sen. *Epp.* 58.36, 70, 77; Cic. *Fin.* 3.16.60–61; and the résumé in Patrizi, *Reg.* 5.22, 7.6.

Book II

wisely, since by death he will put an end not to enjoyment but to torture. Because in doing so he will be
obeying the counsels of the priests, who are God's in-
terpreters,[3] it will be a pious and holy action.

Those who have been persuaded by these arguments
either starve themselves to death[4] or, being put to sleep,
are set free without the sensation of dying.[5] But they
do not make away with anyone against his will, nor in
such a case do they relax in the least their attendance
upon him. They do believe that death counseled by
authority is honorific. But if anyone commits suicide
without having obtained the approval of priests and
senate, they deem him unworthy of either fire or earth
and cast his body ignominiously into a marsh without
proper burial.

Women do not marry till eighteen, men not till they
are four years older.[6] If before marriage a man or woman
is convicted of secret intercourse, he or she is severely
punished,[7] and they are forbidden to marry altogether
unless the governor's pardon remits their guilt. In addition, both father and mother of the family in whose
house the offense was committed incur great disgrace as
having been neglectful in doing their duties. The reason
why they punish this offense so severely is their fore-
knowledge that, unless persons are carefully restrained
from promiscuous intercourse, few will unite in married
love, in which state a whole life must be spent with
one companion[8] and all the troubles incidental to it must
be patiently borne.

3. This is the strongest expression used of priests in *Utopia*.
4. Like Lycurgus (Plut. *Lyc.* 29.5).
5. By means of mandragora (cf. Eras. *Adag.* 3464), or of hemlock,
drunk by Socrates.
6. More's remarks are aimed at too early and too hasty marriages.
7. Cf. Pl. *Rep.* 5.461A. On More's love affairs see Eras. *Ep.*, 4,
17 and More, *Epigr.*, pp. 228–30.
8. Contrast with Socrates' community of wives (*Rep.* 5.457C–D),
defended by More in a rhetorical exercise (Eras. *Ep.*, 4, 21).

In choosing mates, they seriously and strictly espouse a
custom which seemed to us very foolish and extremely
ridiculous. The woman, whether maiden or widow, is
shown naked to the suitor by a worthy and respectable
matron, and similarly the suitor is presented naked before the maiden by a discreet man. We laughed at this
custom and condemned it as foolish. They, on the other
hand, marvelled at the remarkable folly of all other nations. In buying a colt, where there is question of only a
little money, persons are so cautious that though it is
almost bare they will not buy until they have taken off
the saddle and removed all the trappings for fear some
sore[9] lies concealed under these coverings. Yet in the
choice of a wife, an action which will cause either pleasure or disgust to follow them the rest of their lives, they
are so careless that, while the rest of her body is covered
with clothes, they estimate the value of the whole woman
from hardly a single handbreadth of her, only the face
being visible, and clasp her to themselves not without
great danger of their agreeing ill together if something
afterwards gives them offense.

All are not so wise as to regard only the character
of the spouse, and even in the marriages of the wise,
bodily attractions also are no small enhancement to the
virtues of the mind.[10] Certainly such foul deformity may
be hidden beneath these coverings that it may quite
alienate a man's mind from his wife when bodily separation is no longer lawful. If such a deformity arises by
chance after the marriage has been contracted, each person must bear his own fate, but beforehand the laws
ought to protect him from being entrapped by guile.

This provision was the more necessary because the
Utopians are the only people in those parts of the world

9. Erasmus uses the same comparison (*Opera*, 5, 641). The sore
might hint at the detection of venereal disease.
10. Cf. More's "How to Choose a Wife" (*Epigr.*, pp. 181–84).

who are satisfied with one spouse and because matrimony there is seldom broken except by death, unless it be for adultery or for intolerable offensiveness of character. When husband or wife is thus offended, leave is granted by the senate to take another mate.[11] The other party perpetually lives a life of disgrace as well as of celibacy. But they cannot endure the repudiation of an unwilling wife, who is in no way to blame, because some bodily calamity has befallen her. They judge it cruel that a person should be abandoned when most in need of comfort and that old age, since it both entails disease and is a disease itself, should have only an unreliable and weak fidelity.

It sometimes happens, however, that when a married couple agree insufficiently in their dispositions and both find others with whom they hope to live more agreeably, they separate by mutual consent and contract fresh unions, but not without the sanction of the senate. The latter allows of no divorce until its members and their wives have carefully gone into the case. Even then they do not readily give consent because they know that it is a very great drawback to cementing the affection between husband and wife if they have before them the easy hope of a fresh union.

Violators of the conjugal tie are punished by the strictest form of slavery.[12] If both parties are married, the injured parties, provided they consent, are divorced from their adulterous mates and couple together, or else are

11. Erasmus favored a change in ecclesiastical law: not only separation from bed and board but complete severance with right of remarriage (see especially Notes to Matt. 19:3 and I Cor. 7:39 in *Opera*, *6*, 97–98, 692–703).

12. The lax attitude toward adultery is bewailed by many, e.g. Vergil, Brant, Barclay, and especially Erasmus: "Why is it that everywhere simple theft is punished by death and adultery goes almost unscathed (which is in direct contradiction to the laws of all the ancients) . . . ?" (*Prince*, p. 228).

allowed to marry whom they like. But if one of the injured parties continues to feel affection for so undeserving a mate, it is not forbidden to have the marriage continue in force on condition that the party is willing to accompany and share the labor of the other who has been condemned to slavery. Now and then it happens that the penance of the one and the dutiful assiduity of the other move the compassion of the governor and win back their liberty. Relapse into the same offense, however, involves the penalty of death.

For all other crimes there is no law prescribing any fixed penalty, but the punishment is assigned by the senate according to the atrocity, or veniality, of the individual crime. Husbands correct their wives, and parents their children, unless the offense is so serious that it is to the advantage of public morality to have it punished openly. Generally the worst offenses are punished by the sentence of slavery since this prospect, they think, is no less formidable to the criminal and more advantageous to the state than if they make haste to put the offenders to death and get them out of the way at once. Their labor is more profitable than their death, and their example lasts longer to deter others from like crimes. But if they rebel and kick against this treatment, they are thereupon put to death like untameable beasts that cannot be restrained by prison or chain. If they are patient, however, they are not entirely deprived of all hope. When tamed by long and hard punishment, if they show such repentance as testifies that they are more sorry for their sin than for their punishment, then sometimes by the prerogative of the governor and sometimes by the vote of the people their slavery is either lightened or remitted altogether.

To tempt another to an impure act is no less punishable than the commission of that impure act. In every crime the deliberate and avowed attempt is counted equal to the deed, for they think that failure ought not to benefit one who did everything in his power not to fail.

They are very fond of fools.[13] It is a great disgrace to treat them with insult, but there is no prohibition against deriving pleasure from their foolery. The latter, they think, is of the greatest benefit to the fools themselves. If anyone is so stern and morose that he is not amused with anything they either do or say, they do not entrust him with the care of a fool. They fear that he may not treat him with sufficient indulgence since he would find in him neither use nor even amusement, which is his sole faculty.

To deride a man for a disfigurement or the loss of a limb is counted as base and disfiguring, not to the man who is laughed at but to him who laughs, for foolishly upbraiding a man with something as if it were a fault which he was powerless to avoid. While they consider it a sign of a sluggish and feeble mind not to preserve natural beauty, it is, in their judgment, disgraceful affectation to help it out by cosmetics. Experience itself shows them how no elegance of outward form recommends wives to husbands as much as probity and reverence. Some men are attracted only by a handsome shape, but no man's love is kept permanently except by virtue and obedience.

Not merely do they discourage crime by punishment but they offer honors to invite men to virtue. Hence, to great men who have done conspicuous service to their country they set up in the market place statues to stand as a record of noble exploits and, at the same time, to have the glory of forefathers serve their descendants as a spur and stimulus to virtue.

13. As More himself was. Cf. *Works*, pp. 768, 935; *Corresp.*, p. 529; Eras. *Ep.*, 4, 16.

The man who solicits votes to obtain any office is deprived completely of the hope of holding any office at all. They live together in affection and good will. No official is haughty or formidable. They are called fathers and show that character. Honor is paid them willingly, as it should be, and is not exacted from the reluctant. The governor himself is distinguished from citizens not by a robe or a crown but by the carrying of a handful of grain,[14] just as the mark of the high priest is a wax candle borne before him.

They have very few laws because very few are needed for persons so educated. The chief fault they find with other peoples is that almost innumerable books of laws and commentaries are not sufficient. They themselves think it most unfair that any group of men should be bound by laws which are either too numerous to be read through or too obscure to be understood by anyone.

Moreover, they absolutely banish from their country all lawyers, who cleverly manipulate cases and cunningly argue legal points. They consider it a good thing that every man should plead his own cause and say the same to the judge as he would tell his counsel. Thus there is less ambiguity and the truth is more easily elicited when a man, uncoached in deception by a lawyer, conducts his own case and the judge skillfully weighs each statement and helps untutored minds to defeat the false accusations of the crafty. To secure these advantages in other countries is difficult, owing to the immense mass of extremely complicated laws. But with the Utopians each man is expert in law. First, they have, as I said, very few laws and, secondly, they regard the most obvious interpretation of the law as the most fair interpretation.

This policy follows from their reasoning that, since

14. Cf. the letter to Erasmus where More speaks of being crowned with a diadem of wheat (*S.L.*, p. 85). On the significance of royal insignia see Erasmus, *Folly*, p. 95.

all laws are promulgated to remind every man of his duty, the more recondite interpretation reminds only very few (for there are few who can arrive at it) whereas the more simple and obvious sense of the laws is open to all. Otherwise, what difference would it make for the common people, who are the most numerous and also most in need of instruction, whether you framed no law at all or whether the interpretation of the law you framed was such that no one could elicit it except by great ingenuity and long argument? Now, the untrained judgment of the common people cannot attain to the meaning of such an interpretation nor can their lives be long enough, seeing that they are wholly taken up with getting a living.

These virtues of the Utopians have spurred their neighbors (who are free and independent since many of them were long ago delivered from tyrants by the Utopians) to obtain officials from them, some for one year and others for five years.[15] On the expiration of their office they escort them home with honor and praise and bring back successors with them to their own country. Certainly these peoples make very good and wholesome provision for the commonwealth. Seeing that the latter's prosperity or ruin depends on the character of officials, of whom could they have made a wiser choice than of those who cannot be drawn from the path of honor by any bribe since it is no good to them as they will shortly return home, nor influenced by crooked partiality or animosity toward any since they are strangers to the citizens? These two evils, favoritism and avarice, wherever they have settled in men's judgments, instantly destroy all justice, the strongest sinew of the commonwealth. The nations who seek their administrators from Utopia are

15. Suggested perhaps by Plato's Athenian Academy for future administrators.

called allies by them; the name of friend is reserved for all the others whom they have benefited.[16]

Treaties which all other nations so often conclude among themselves, break, and renew, they never make with any nation. "What is the use of a treaty," they ask, "as though nature of herself did not sufficiently bind one man to another? If a person does not regard nature, do you suppose he will care anything about words?"

They are led to this opinion chiefly because in those parts of the world treaties and alliances between kings are not observed with much good faith.[17] In Europe, however, and especially in those parts where the faith and religion of Christ prevails, the majesty of treaties is everywhere holy and inviolable, partly through the justice and goodness of kings, partly through the reverence and fear of the Sovereign Pontiffs. Just as the latter themselves undertake nothing which they do not most conscientiously perform,[18] so they command all other rulers to abide by their promises in every way and compel the recalcitrant by pastoral censure and severe reproof. Popes are perfectly right, of course, in thinking it a most disgraceful thing that those who are specially called the faithful should not faithfully adhere to their commitments.

But in that new world, which is almost as far removed from ours by the equator as their life and character are different from ours, there is no trust in treaties. The more numerous and holy the ceremonies with which a treaty

16. A *socius,* 'ally,' was always an *amicus,* 'friend,' but not vice versa.

17. "The foundation of justice . . . is good faith—that is, truth and fidelity to promises and agreements" (Cic. *Off.* 1.7.23). Cf. Erasmus, *Prince,* p. 239, and Elyot, *Gou.* 3.7.

18. An ironic comment on the diplomacy of Julius II and his predecessor, Alexander VI, of whom Machiavelli writes: "the greater the oaths with which he made a promise, the less he observed it" (*Prince* 18).

is struck the more quickly is it broken. They find some defect in the wording, which sometimes they cunningly devise of set purpose, so that they can never be held by such strong bonds as not somehow to escape from them and break both the treaty and their faith. If this cunning, nay fraud and deceit, were found to have occurred in the contracts of private persons, the treaty-makers with great disdain would exclaim against it as sacrilegious and meriting the gallows—though the very same men plume themselves on being the authors of such advice when given to kings.

In consequence men think either that all justice is only a plebeian and low virtue which is far below the majesty of kings or that there are at least two forms of it: the one which goes on foot and creeps on the ground, fit only for the common sort and bound by many chains so that it can never overstep its barriers; the other a virtue of kings, which, as it is more august than that of ordinary folk, is also far freer so that everything is permissible to it—except what it finds disagreeable.

This behavior, as I said, of rulers there who keep their treaties so badly is, I suppose, the reason why the Utopians make none; if they lived here, they would perhaps change their minds. Nevertheless they believe that, though treaties are faithfully observed, it is a pity that the custom of making them at all had grown up. The result (as though peoples which are divided by the slight interval of a hill or a river were joined by no bond of nature) is men's persuasion that they are born one another's adversaries and enemies and that they are right in aiming at one another's destruction except in so far as treaties prevent it. What is more, even when treaties are made, friendship does not grow up but the license of freebooting continues to the extent that, for lack of skill in drawing up the treaty, no sufficient precaution to prevent this activity has been included in the articles. But the Utopians, on the contrary, think that nobody who has done you no harm should be accounted an enemy, that the fellowship created by nature takes the place of a treaty, and that men are better and more firmly joined together by good will than by pacts, by spirit than by words.

MILITARY AFFAIRS

War, as an activity fit only for beasts and yet practiced by no kind of beast so constantly as by man, they regard with utter loathing.[1] Against the usage of almost all nations they count nothing so inglorious as glory sought in war. Nevertheless men and women alike assiduously exercise themselves in military training on fixed days lest they should be unfit for war when need requires.[2] Yet they do not lightly go to war. They do so only to protect their own territory or to drive an invading enemy out of their friends' lands or, in pity for a people oppressed by tyranny, to deliver them by force of arms from the yoke and slavery of the tyrant, a course prompted by human sympathy.

They oblige their friends with help, not always indeed to defend them merely but sometimes also to requite and avenge injuries previously done to them. They act, however, only if they themselves are consulted before any step is taken and if they themselves initiate the war after they have approved the cause and demanded restitution in vain.[3] They take the final step of war not only

1. There is a rather common play on the conjectural derivation of *bellum*, 'war,' from *belua*, 'beast,' (e.g. in Eras. *Adag.* 3001). Mercenaries were called *beluae* in Book I. A "universal peace" was one of More's three most ardent wishes (Harpsfield, p. 68).

2. The citizens' militia in Utopia, as in England, contrasts with the professional army in Plato's republic (*Rep.* 2.370B, 2.374B–D, 4.423A) and in Sparta (Plut. *Lyc.* 4.5).

3. A requisite for a just war according to the fetial code of the Romans (cf. Cic. *Off.* 1.11.36).

when a hostile inroad has carried off booty but also much more fiercely when the merchants among their friends undergo unjust persecution under the color of justice in any other country, either on the pretext of laws in themselves unjust or by the distortion of laws in themselves good.

Such was the origin of the war which the Utopians had waged a little before our time on behalf of the Nephelogetes[4] against the Alaopolitans.[5] The Nephelogetic traders suffered a wrong, as they thought, under pretence of law, but whether right or wrong, it was avenged by a fierce war. Into this war the neighboring nations brought their energies and resources to assist the power and to intensify the rancor of both sides. Most flourishing nations were either shaken to their foundations or grievously afflicted. The troubles upon troubles that arose were ended only by the enslavement and surrender of the Alaopolitans. Since the Utopians were not fighting in their own interest, they yielded them into the power of the Nephelogetes, a people who, when the Alaopolitans were prosperous, were not in the least comparable to them.

So severely do the Utopians punish wrong done to their friends, even in money matters—but not wrongs done to themselves. When they lose their goods anywhere through fraud, but without personal violence, their anger goes no further than abstention from trade with that nation until satisfaction is made. The reason is not that they care less for their citizens than their allies. They are more grieved at their allies' pecuniary loss than their own because their friends' merchants suffer severely by the loss as it falls on their private property, but their own citizens lose nothing but what comes

4. 'Cloud-born.'
5. 'Peopleless citizens,' i.e. 'citizens without a country' or 'citizens in a city without people.'

from the common stock and what was plentiful and, as it were, superfluous at home—or else it would not have been exported. As a result, the loss is not felt by any individual. They consider it excessively cruel to avenge such a loss by the death of many when the disadvantage of the loss affects neither the life nor the subsistence of any of their own people.

If a Utopian citizen, however, is wrongfully disabled or killed anywhere, whether the plot is due to the government or to a private citizen, they first ascertain the facts by an embassy and then, if the guilty persons are not surrendered, they cannot be appeased but forthwith declare war. If the guilty persons are surrendered, they are punished either with death or with enslavement.

They not only regret but blush at a victory that has cost much bloodshed, thinking it folly to purchase wares, however precious, too dear. If they overcome and crush the enemy by stratagem and cunning,[6] they feel great pride and celebrate a public triumph over the victory and put up a trophy as for a strenuous exploit. They boast themselves as having acted with valor and heroism whenever their victory is such as no animal except man could have won, that is, by strength of intellect; for, by strength of body, say they, bears, lions, boars, wolves, dogs, and other wild beasts are wont to fight. Most of them are superior to us in brawn and fierceness, but they are all inferior in cleverness and calculation.

Their one and only object in war is to secure that which, had it been obtained beforehand, would have prevented the declaration of war. If that is out of the question, they require such severe punishment of those on whom they lay the blame that for the future they may be afraid to attempt anything of the same sort.

6. The Macedonians under Philip, the Carthaginians, and the Numidians are classic examples.

Book II

These are their chief interests in the enterprise, which they set about promptly to secure, yet taking more care to avoid danger than to win praise or fame.

The moment war is declared,[7] they arrange that simultaneously a great number of placards, made more effective by bearing their public seal, should be set up secretly in the most prominent spots of enemy territory. Herein they promise huge rewards to anyone who will kill the enemy king. Further, they offer smaller sums, but those considerable, for the heads of the individuals whose names they specify in the same proclamations. These are the men whom, next to the king himself, they regard as responsible for the hostile measures taken against them. Whatever reward they fix for an assassin, they double for the man who brings any of the denounced parties alive to them. They actually offer the same rewards, with a guarantee of personal safety, to the persons proscribed, if they will turn against their fellows.

So it swiftly comes about that their enemies suspect all outsiders and, in addition, neither trust nor are loyal to one another. They are in a state of utter panic and no less peril. It is well known that it has often happened that many of them, and especially the king himself, have been betrayed by those in whom they had placed the greatest trust, so easily do bribes incite men to commit every kind of crime. They are boundless in their offers of reward. Remembering, however, what a risk they invite the man to run, they take care that the greatness of the peril is balanced by the extent of the rewards. In consequence they promise and faithfully pay down not only an immense amount of gold but also landed prop-

7. What follows comments ironically on actual practices in Europe. To the Utopians the enemy prince appears as a tyrant against whom tyrannicide is licit. More has a Latin translation of Lucian's *Tyrannicide* and several epigrams about tyrants (*Epigr.*, pp. 161–62, 171–75, 180–81, 190, 217).

erty with high income in very secure places in the territory of friends.

This habit of bidding for and purchasing an enemy, which is elsewhere condemned as the cruel deed of a degenerate nature, they think reflects great credit, first on their wisdom because they thus bring to a conclusion great wars without any battle at all, and secondly on their humanity and mercy because by the death of a few guilty people they purchase the lives of many harmless persons who would have fallen in battle, both on their own side and that of the enemy. They are almost as sorry for the throng and mass of the enemy as for their own citizens. They know that the common folk do not go to war of their own accord but are driven to it by the madness of kings.

If this plan does not succeed, they sow the seeds of dissension broadcast and foster strife by leading a brother of the king or one of the noblemen to hope that he may obtain the throne. If internal strife dies down, then they stir up and involve the neighbors of their enemies by reviving some forgotten claims to dominion such as kings have always at their disposal. Promising their own assistance for the war, they supply money liberally but are very chary of sending their own citizens. They hold them so singularly dear and regard one another of such value that they would not care to exchange any of their own people for the king of the opposite party. As to gold and silver, since they keep it all for this one use, they pay it out without any reluctance, for they would live just as well if they spent it all. Moreover, in addition to the riches which they keep at home, they have also a vast treasure abroad in that many nations, as I said before, are in their debt.

With the riches, they hire and send to war soldiers from all parts, but especially from among the Zapole-

tans.[8] These people live five hundred miles to the east of
Utopia and are fearsome, rough, and wild. They prefer
their own rugged woods and mountains among which
they are bred. They are a hard race, capable of enduring
heat, cold, and toil, lacking all refinements, engaging in
no farming, careless about the houses they live in and
the clothes they wear, and occupied only with their
flocks and herds. To a great extent they live by hunting
and plundering. They are born for warfare and zealously
seek an opportunity for fighting. When they find it, they
eagerly embrace it. Leaving the country in great force,
they offer themselves at a cheap rate to anyone who needs
fighting men. The only trade they know in life is that
by which they seek their death.

They fight with ardor and incorruptible loyalty for
those from whom they receive their pay. Yet they
bind themselves for no fixed period but take sides on
such terms that the next day when higher pay is offered
them, even by the enemy, they take his side, and then
the day after, if a trifle more is offered to tempt them
back, return to the side they took at first.

In almost every war that breaks out there are many
of them in both armies. It is a daily occurrence that
men connected by ties of blood, who were hired on the
same side and so became intimate with one another,
soon afterward are separated into two hostile forces and
meet in battle. Forgetting both kinship and friendship,
they run one another through with the utmost ferocity.
They are driven to mutual destruction for no other
reason than that they are hired by opposing kings for
a tiny sum of which they take such careful account that
they are readily induced to change sides by the addition
of a penny to their daily rate of pay. So have they

8. 'Busy sellers,' i.e. sellers and resellers of their services. They are
to be identified as the Swiss.

speedily aquired a habit of avarice which nevertheless profits them not one whit. What they get by exposing their lives they spend instantly in debauchery and that of a dreary sort.

This people will battle for the Utopians against any mortals whatsoever because their service is hired at a rate higher than they could get anywhere else. The Utopians, just as they seek good men to use them, so enlist these villains to abuse them. When need requires, they thrust them under the tempting bait of great promises into greatest perils. Generally a large proportion never returns to claim payment, but the survivors are honestly paid what has been promised them to incite them again to like deeds of daring. The Utopians do not care in the least how many Zapoletans they lose, thinking that they would be the greatest benefactors to the human race if they could relieve the world of all the dregs of this abominable and impious people.[9]

Next to them they employ the forces of the people for whom they are fighting and then auxiliary squadrons of all their other friends. Last of all they add a contingent of their own citizens out of which they appoint some man of tried valor to command the whole army. For him they have two substitutes who hold no rank as long as he is safe. But if he is captured or killed, the first of the two becomes as it were his heir and successor, and he, if events require, is succeeded by the third. They thus avoid the disorganization of the whole army through the endangering of the commander, the fortunes of war being always incalculable.

9. In an interview with Henry VIII in 1516, Sebastian Giustinian "dilated on the inhumanity of the Germans, who burn, destroy, and kill in all directions; the ferocity of the Swiss was notorious, and no sex or age was exempt from their inhumanity" (LP, 2, No. 1991).

Book II

In each city a choice is made among those who volunteer. No one is driven to fight abroad against his will because they are convinced that if anyone is somewhat timorous by nature, he not only will not acquit himself manfully but will throw fear into his companions. Should any war, however, assail their own country, they put the fainthearted, if physically fit, on shipboard mixed among the braver sort or put them here and there to man the walls where they cannot run away. Thus, shame at being seen to flinch by their own side, the close quarters with the enemy, and the withdrawal of hope of escape combine to overpower their timidity, and often they make a virtue of extreme necessity.

Just as no one of the men is made to go to a foreign war against his will, so if the women are anxious to accompany their husbands on military service, not only do they not forbid them but actually encourage them and incite them by expressions of praise. When they have gone out, they are placed alongside their husbands on the battle front. Each man is surrounded by his own children and relations by marriage and blood so that those may be closest and lend one another mutual assistance whom nature most impels to help one another. It is the greatest reproach for one spouse to return without the other or for a son to come back having lost his parent. The result is that, when it comes to hand-to-hand fighting, if the enemy stands his ground, the battle is long and anguished and ends with mutual extermination.

As I have said, they take every care not to be obliged to fight in person as long as they can finish the war by the assistance of hired substitutes. When personal service is inevitable, they are as courageous in fighting as they were ingenious in avoiding it as long as they might. They are not fierce in the first onslaught, but their strength increases by degrees through their slow and hard resistance. Their spirit is so stubborn that they would rather be cut to pieces than give way.[10] The absence of anxiety about livelihood at home, as well as the removal of that worry which troubles men about the future of their families (for such solicitude everywhere breaks the highest courage), makes their spirit exalted and disdainful of defeat.

Moreover, their expert training in military discipline gives them confidence. Finally, their good and sound opinions, in which they have been trained from childhood both by teaching and by the good institutions of their country, give them additional courage. So they do not hold their life so cheap as recklessly to throw it away and not so immoderately dear as greedily and shamefully to hold fast to it when honor bids them give it up.

While the battle is everywhere most hot, a band of picked youths who have taken an oath to devote themselves to the task hunt out the opposing general. They openly attack him; they secretly ambush him. They assail him both from far and from near. A long and continuous wedge[11] of men, fresh comers constantly taking the place of those exhausted, keeps up the attack. It seldom happens, unless he look to his safety by running away, that he is not killed or does not fall alive into the enemy's hands.

If the victory rests with them, there is no indiscriminate carnage, for they would rather take the routed as prisoners than kill them. They never pursue the fleeing enemy without keeping one division all the time drawn up ready for engagement under their banners. To such

10. This spirit established the greatness of Rome (Sall. *Cat.* 7–9) and Sparta (Eras. *Adag.* 2410). More later declared: "for dread of death and torment, . . . to run quite away . . . is by the law of arms reputed a very shameful and traitorous act" (*Works*, p. 1356).

11. Used by the Germans (Tac. *Germ.* 6) and discussed by Vegetius (*Mil.* 3).

an extent is this the case that if, after the rest of the army has been beaten, they win the victory by this last reserve force, they prefer to let all their enemies escape rather than get into the habit of pursuing them with their own ranks in disorder.[12] They remember that more than once it has happened to themselves that, when the great bulk of their army has been beaten and routed and when the enemy, flushed with victory, has been chasing the fugitives in all directions, a few of their number, held in reserve and ready for emergencies, have suddenly attacked the scattered and straying enemy who, feeling themselves quite safe, were off their guard. Thereby they have changed the whole fortune of the battle and, wresting out of the enemy's hands a certain and undoubted victory, have, though conquered, conquered their conquerors in turn.

It is not easy to say whether they are more cunning in laying ambushes or more cautious in avoiding them. You would think they contemplated flight when that is the very last thing intended; but, on the other hand, when they do determine to flee, you would imagine that they were thinking of anything but that. If they feel themselves to be inferior in number or in position, either by night they noiselessly march and move their camp or evade the enemy by some stratagem, or else by day they retire so imperceptibly and in such regular order that it is as dangerous to attack them in retreat as it would be in advance. They protect their camp most carefully by a deep and broad ditch, the earth taken out of it being thrown inside. They do not utilize the labor of the lowest workmen for the purpose, but the soldiers do it with their own hands. The whole army is set at work,

12. "He who rashly pursues a flying enemy with troops in disorder, seems bent upon throwing away that victory which he had before obtained" (Vegetius, *Mil.* 3). The heavy-armed infantry kept ranks and left the pursuit to light-armed troops and cavalry.

except those who watch under arms in front of the rampart in case of emergencies. Thus, through the efforts of so many, they complete great fortifications, enclosing a large space, with incredible speed.

They wear armor strong enough to turn blows but easily adapted to all motions and gestures of the body. They do not feel any awkwardness even in swimming, for they practice swimming under arms as part of their apprenticeship in military discipline. The weapons they use at a distance are arrows,[13] which they shoot with great strength and sureness of aim not only on foot but also on horseback. At close quarters they use not swords but battle-axes[14] which, because of their sharp point and great weight, are deadly weapons, whether employed for thrusting or hacking. They are very clever in inventing war machines.[15] They hide them, when made, with the greatest care lest, if made known before required by circumstances, they be rather a laughingstock than an instrument of war. In making them, their first object is to have them easy to carry and handy to pivot.

If a truce is made with the enemy, they keep it so religiously as not to break it even under provocation. They do not ravage the enemy's territory nor burn his crops. Rather, they do not even allow them to be trodden down by the feet of men or horses, as far as can be, thinking that they grow for their own benefit. They injure no noncombatant unless he is a spy. When cities are surrendered to them, they keep them intact. They

13. Fortescue declared that England's "might standeth most upon archers" (*Gov.*, p. 137). Parliamentary acts in 1511–12 and 1514–15 tried to promote archery, which Elyot later called "the principal of all other exercises" (*Gou.* 1.27). The mounted archers of Parthia were especially renowned.

14. Pikes and halberds, especially in massed columns (as with the Swiss), were dangerous and effective at this time.

15. Artillery and small arms were being extensively developed by 1516, but there is no mention of gun and powder in *Utopia*.

do not plunder even those which they have stormed but put to death the men who prevented surrender and make slaves of the rest of the defenders. They leave unharmed the crowd of noncombatants. If they find out that any persons recommended the surrender of the town, they give them a share of the property of the condemned. They present their auxiliaries with the rest of the confiscated goods, but not a single one of their own men gets any of the booty.

When the war is over, they do not charge the expense against their friends, for whom they have borne the cost, but against the conquered. Under this head they make them not only pay money, which they lay aside for similar warlike purposes, but also surrender estates, from which they may enjoy forever a large annual income. In many countries they have such revenues which, coming little by little from various sources, have grown to the sum of over seven hundred thousand ducats[16] a year. To these estates they dispatch some of their own citizens under the title of Financial Agents to live there in great style and to play the part of magnates. Yet much is left over to put into the public treasury, unless they prefer to give the conquered nation credit. They often do the latter until they need to use the money, and even then it scarcely ever happens that they call in the whole sum. From these estates they confer a share on those who at their request undertake the dangerous mission which I have previously described.

If any king takes up arms against them and prepares to invade their territory, they at once meet him in great strength beyond their borders. They never lightly make war in their own country nor is any emergency so pressing as to compel them to admit foreign auxiliaries into their island.

16. About £327,000, with many times the present-day value.

Utopia

UTOPIAN RELIGIONS

There are different kinds of religion[1] not only on the island as a whole but also in each city. Some worship as god the sun, others the moon, others one of the planets.[2] There are some who reverence a man conspicuous for either virtue or glory in the past not only as god but even as the supreme god. But by far the majority, and those by far the wiser, believe in nothing of the kind but in a certain single being, unknown,[3] eternal, immense, inexplicable, far above the reach of the human mind, diffused throughout the universe not in mass but in power. Him they call father. To him alone they attribute the beginnings, the growth, the increase, the changes, and the ends of all things as they have perceived them. To no other do they give divine honors.

In addition, all the other Utopians too, though varying in their beliefs, agree with them in this respect that they hold there is one supreme being, to whom are due both the creation and the providential government of the whole world.[4] All alike call him Mithras[5] in their

1. Utopian religion is predominantly natural; i.e. its truths are reached mainly by reason independently of divine revelation. More later writes: "there is a God, which thou not only believest by faith, but also knowest by reason" (*Works*, p. 76; cf. p. 128).

2. The Book of Wisdom (Chaps. 13–14) condemns idolaters but somewhat excuses adorers of heavenly bodies. The latter were worshipped on Iambulus' islands of the sun (Diod. Sic. 2.59.2, 2.59.7).

3. "God is distinguished by us from other things by the very fact that we know of him what he is *not*" (Aquinas, *In Boet. de Trin.* q. 2, a. 2, ad 2).

4. "All the whole number of the old philosophers . . . found out by nature and reason that there was a God, either maker or governor or both, of all this whole engine of the world" (More, *Works*, pp. 128–29).

5. The Utopians, although Greek in origin, have a Persian language and use the name of the Persian god, Mithras, the numerical value of whose name equals 360, roughly the number of days it takes the sun to complete its cycle.

native language, but in this respect they disagree, that he is looked on differently by different persons. Each professes that whatever that is which he regards as supreme is that very same nature to whose unique power and majesty the sum of all things is attributed by the common consent of all nations. But gradually they are all beginning to depart from this medley of superstitions and are coming to unite in that one religion which seems to surpass the rest in reasonableness.[6] Nor is there any doubt that the other beliefs would all have disappeared long ago had not whatever untoward event, that happened to anyone when he was deliberating on a change of religion, been construed by fear as not having happened by chance but as having been sent from heaven—as if the deity whose worship he was forsaking were thus avenging an intention so impious against himself.[7]

But after they had heard from us the name of Christ,[8] His teaching, His character, His miracles, and the no less wonderful constancy of the many martyrs whose blood freely shed had drawn so many nations far and wide into their fellowship, you would not believe how readily disposed they, too, were to join it, whether through the rather mysterious inspiration of God or because they thought it nearest to that belief which has the widest prevalence among them. But I think that this factor, too, was of no small weight, that they had heard that His disciples' common way of life had been pleasing

6. The truest natural religion has to surpass all others in reasonableness just as in philosophy, which uses reasons, no system, according to reason, can be found truer than hedonism.

7. About *The City of God,* Augustine explains: "The first five books . . . are a refutation of their position who maintain . . . that the prohibition of it [the worship of many gods] is the source and origin of calamities such as the fall of Rome" (*Retract.* 2.43).

8. "Unto all such paynims as in any place lived naturally well and kept themself from idolatry, God sent the faith of Christ to keep them from hell" (More, *Works,* p. 1282).

to Christ [9] and that it is still in use among the truest
societies of Christians.[10] But whatever it was that influenced them, not a few joined our religion and were
cleansed by the holy water of baptism.

But because among us four (for that was all that was
left, two of our group having succumbed to fate) there
was, I am sorry to say, no priest, they were initiated in
all other matters, but so far they lack those sacraments
which with us only priests administer.[11] They understand, however, what they are, and desire them with the
greatest eagerness. Moreover, they are even debating
earnestly among themselves whether, without the dispatch of a Christian bishop, one chosen out of their own
number might receive the sacerdotal character.[12] It
seemed that they would choose a candidate, but by the
time of my departure they had not yet done so.

Even those who do not agree with the religion of
Christ do not try to deter others from it. They do not
attack any who have made their profession. Only one
of our company, while I was there, was interfered with.
As soon as he was baptized, in spite of our advice to the
contrary, he spoke publicly of Christ's religion with
more zeal than discretion. He began to grow so warm
in his preaching that not only did he prefer our worship
to any other but he condemned all the rest outright. He
proclaimed them to be profane in themselves and their

9. Cf. Acts 2:44–45, 4:32–35, and More, *Corresp.*, p. 195.

10. Religious orders. Cf. Augustine's monastic rule: "you must
have everything in common" (*Ep.* 211, *PL, 33,* 960).

11. Bishops are the ordinary ministers of confirmation and holy
orders; priests, of the eucharist, penance, and extreme unction.

12. "A character . . . is a spiritual seal or stamp impressed on
the soul by God to indicate the consecration of that soul to him
in some official capacity. . . . Order bestows the power and office
of *dispensing* and *ministering* them [divine gifts] to the faithful"
(G. D. Smith, ed., *Teaching of the Catholic Church,* 2 [New York,
1949], 1030).

followers to be impious and sacrilegious and worthy of everlasting fire. When he had long been preaching in this style, they arrested him, tried him, and convicted him not for despising their religion but for stirring up a riot among the people. His sentence after the verdict of guilty was exile. Actually, they count this principle among their most ancient institutions, that no one should suffer for his religion.

Utopus had heard that before his arrival the inhabitants had been continually quarreling among themselves about religion. He had observed that the universal dissensions between the individual sects who were fighting for their country had given him the opportunity of overcoming them all. From the very beginning, therefore, after he had gained the victory, he especially ordained that it should be lawful for every man to follow the religion of his choice, that each might strive to bring others over to his own, provided that he quietly and modestly supported his own by reasons nor bitterly demolished all others if his persuasions were not successful nor used any violence and refrained from abuse. If a person contends too vehemently in expressing his views, he is punished with exile or enslavement.

Utopus laid down these regulations not merely from regard for peace, which he saw to be utterly destroyed by constant wrangling and implacable hatred, but because he thought that this method of settlement was in the interest of religion itself. On religion he did not venture rashly to dogmatize. He was uncertain whether God did not desire a varied and manifold worship[13] and therefore did not inspire different people with different views. But he was certain in thinking it both insolence and folly to demand by violence and threats

13. Variety of worship, "according to God's ordination, perhaps begets a certain wonderful glory in the universe" (Ficino, *Opera* [Basel, 1576], *1*, 4).

that all should think to be true what you believe to be true. Moreover, even if it should be the case that one single religion is true and all the rest are false, he readily foresaw that, provided the matter was handled reasonably and moderately, truth by its own natural force would finally emerge sooner or later and stand forth conspicuously. But if the struggle were decided by arms and riots, since the worst men are always the most unyielding, the best and holiest religion would be overwhelmed because of the conflicting false religions, like grain choked by thorns and underbrush.[14]

So he made the whole matter of religion an open question and left each one free to choose what he should believe. By way of exception, he conscientiously and strictly gave injunction that no one should fall so far below the dignity of human nature as to believe that souls likewise perish with the body[15] or that the world is the mere sport of chance and not governed by any divine providence.[16] After this life, accordingly, vices are ordained to be punished and virtue rewarded. Such is their belief, and if anyone thinks otherwise, they do not regard him even as a member of mankind, seeing that he has lowered the lofty nature of his soul to the level of a beast's miserable body—so far are they from classing him among their citizens whose laws and cus-

14. With the removal of violence and force "would I little doubt but that the good seed, being sown among the people, should as well come up and be as strong to save itself as the cockle" (More, *Works*, p. 275). Cf. Matt. 13:7, 13:22; Mark 4:7, 4:18–19; Luke 8:7, 8:14.

15. The immortality of the soul is one of the main mysteries of the Christian faith (More, *Corresp.*, p. 12), yet More blames "such as have so far fallen from the nature of man into a brutish beastly persuasion as to believe that soul and body die both at once" (*Works*, p. 315).

16. "The marvelous beauty and constant course whereof [of the world] showeth well that it neither was made nor governed by chance" (More, *Works*, p. 129).

toms he would treat as worthless if it were not for fear. Who can doubt that he will strive either to evade by craft the public laws of his country or to break them by violence in order to serve his own private desires when he has nothing to fear but laws and no hope beyond the body?

Therefore an individual of this mind is tendered no honor, is entrusted with no office, and is put in charge of no function. He is universally regarded as of a sluggish and low disposition. But they do not punish him in any way,[17] being convinced that it is in no man's power to believe what he chooses, nor do they compel him by threats to disguise his views, nor do they allow in the matter any deceptions or lies which they hate exceedingly as being next door to calculated malice. They forbid him to argue in support of his opinion in the presence of the common people, but in private before the priests and important personages they not only permit but also encourage it, being sure that such madness will in the end give way to reason.

There are others, too, and these not a few, who are not interfered with because they do not altogether lack reason for their view and because they are not evil men. By a much different error, these believe that brute animals also have immortal souls,[18] but not comparable to ours in dignity or destined to equal felicity. Almost all Utopians are absolutely certain and convinced that human bliss will be so immense that, while they lament every man's illness, they regret the death of no one but him whom they see torn from life anxiously and unwillingly. This behavior they take to be a very bad omen

17. The essential note of heresy is not error but obstinacy in error. Punishment in Utopia, although not physical as in Europe, is in fact severe: public infamy, exclusion from office, and forced silence in public.

18. This theory was held mainly by Pythagoreans and Platonists.

as though the soul, being without hope and having a guilty conscience, dreaded its departure through a secret premonition of impending punishment. Besides, they suppose that God will not be pleased with the coming of one who, when summoned, does not gladly hasten to obey but is reluctantly drawn against his will. Persons who behold this kind of death are filled with horror and therefore carry the dead out to burial in melancholy silence. Then, after praying God to be merciful to their shades and graciously to pardon their infirmities, they cover the corpse with earth.[19]

On the other hand, when men have died cheerfully and full of good hope, no one mourns for them, but they accompany their funerals with song, with great affection commending their souls to God. Then, with reverence rather than with sorrow, they cremate the bodies. On the spot they erect a pillar on which are inscribed the good points of the deceased. On returning home they recount his character and his deeds. No part of his life is more frequently or more gladly spoken of than his cheerful death.

They judge that this remembrance of uprightness is not only a most efficacious means of stimulating the living to good deeds but also a most acceptable form of attention to the dead. The latter they think are present when they are talked about, though invisible to the dull sight of mortals. It would be inconsistent with the lot of the blessed not to be able to travel freely where they please,[20] and it would be ungrateful of them to reject absolutely all desire of revisiting their friends to

19. The reason for inhumation is obscure. Both burial and cremation were customary in Greece and Rome, apparently without difference in belief. Cremation was not practised by the Persians, with whose language the Utopian has an affinity.

20. "When saints were in this world at liberty and might walk the world about, ween we that in heaven they stand tied to a post?" (More, *Works*, p. 188).

Book II

whom they were bound during their lives by mutual
love and charity. Charity, like all other good things,
they conjecture to be increased after death rather than
diminished in all good men. Consequently they believe
that the dead move about among the living and are witnesses of their words and actions. Hence they go about
their business with more confidence because of reliance
on such protection. The belief, moreover, in the personal presence of their forefathers keeps men from any
secret dishonorable deed.

They utterly despise and deride auguries and all other
divinations of vain superstition, to which great attention
is paid in other countries. But miracles, which occur
without the assistance of nature, they venerate as operations and witnesses of the divine power at work.[21] In
their country, too, they say, miracles often occur. Sometimes in great and critical affairs they pray publicly for
a miracle, which they very confidently look for and
obtain.

They think that the investigation of nature, with the
praise arising from it, is an act of worship acceptable
to God. There are persons, however, and these not so
very few, who for religious motives eschew learning and
scientific pursuit and yet allow themselves no leisure.[22]
It is only by keeping busy and by all good offices that
they are determined to merit the happiness coming after
death. Some tend the sick. Others repair roads, clean
out ditches, rebuild bridges, dig turf and sand and stone,
fell and cut up trees, and transport wood, grain, and
other things into the cities in carts. Not only for the

21. Miracles can prove, not only the true church (More, *Works*,
pp. 201, 455; *Corresp.*, p. 334), but also a particular doctrine, e.g.
divine providence; hence miracles can happen among non-Chris-
tians (cf. Aquinas, *De pot.* q. 6, a. 5; *S.T.* 2-2, q. 178, a. 2, ad 3).
22. The ascetic ideal here contrasts with the idle life charged
against European religious in Book I.

public but also for private persons they behave as servants and as more than slaves.

If anywhere there is a task so rough, hard, and filthy that most are deterred from it by the toil, disgust, and despair involved, they gladly and cheerfully claim it all for themselves. While perpetually engaged in hard work themselves, they secure leisure for the others and yet claim no credit for it. They neither belittle insultingly the life of others nor extol their own.[23] The more that these men put themselves in the position of slaves the more are they honored by all.

Of these persons there are two schools. The one is composed of celibates[24] who not only eschew all sexual activity but also abstain from eating flesh meat and in some cases from eating all animal food. They entirely reject the pleasures of this life as harmful. They long only for the future life by means of their watching and sweat. Hoping to obtain it very soon, they are cheerful and active in the meantime.

The other school[25] is just as fond of hard labor, but regards matrimony as preferable, not despising the comfort which it brings and thinking that their duty to nature requires them to perform the marital act and their duty to the country to beget children. They avoid no pleasure unless it interferes with their labor. They like flesh meat just because they think that this fare makes them stronger for any work whatsoever. The Utopians regard these men as the saner but the first-named as the holier. If the latter based upon arguments from reason their preference of celibacy to matrimony

23. A charge made frequently against contemporary religious, who were proud and sensitive about their vocation and their order.

24. Chastity is "a great gift" but not "a seldom gift" (More, *Works*, p. 231).

25. Roughly equivalent to a Third Order, i.e. persons living in the world but following the rule of St. Francis, St. Dominic, etc., as far as possible.

and of a hard life to a comfortable one, they would laugh them to scorn. Now, however, since they say they are prompted by religion, they look up to and reverence them. For there is nothing about which they are more careful than not lightly to dogmatize on any point of religion. Such, then, are the men whom in their language they call by a special name of their own, Buthrescae,[26] a word which may be translated as "religious par excellence."

They have priests of extraordinary holiness, and therefore very few. They have no more than thirteen[27] in each city—with a like number of churches—except when they go to war. In that case, seven go forth with the army, and the same number of substitutes is appointed for the interval. When the regular priests come back, everyone returns to his former duties. Then those who are above the number of thirteen, until they succeed to the places of those who die, attend upon the high priest in the meantime. One, you see, is appointed to preside over the rest. They are elected by the people, just as all the other officials are,[28] by secret ballot to avoid party spirit. When elected, they are ordained by their own group.

They preside over divine worship, order religious rites, and are censors of morals.[29] It is counted a great disgrace for a man to be summoned or rebuked by them as not being of upright life. It is their function to give advice and admonition, but to check and punish offenders belongs to the governor and the other civil officials. The

26. 'Extraordinarily religious.'

27. Apparently one bishop and twelve priests, possibly suggested by Christ and the twelve apostles.

28. This is possibly a protest against increasing nomination by secular princes.

29. By omission or silence, the clergy are seen to be excluded from civil office, the holding of which would prevent them, as it did European ecclesiastics, from performing their spiritual duties.

priests, however, do exclude from divine services persons whom they find to be unusually bad. There is almost no punishment which is more dreaded: they incur very great disgrace and are tortured by a secret fear of religion. Even their bodies will not long go scot-free. If they do not demonstrate to the priests their speedy repentance, they are seized and punished by the senate for their impiety.

To the priests is entrusted the education of children and youths. They regard concern for their morals and virtue as no less important than for their advancement in learning. They take the greatest pains from the very first to instill into children's minds, while still tender and pliable, good opinions, which are also useful for the preservation of their commonwealth. When once they are firmly implanted in children, they accompany them all through their adult lives and are of great help in watching over the condition of the commonwealth. The latter never decays except through vices which arise from wrong attitudes.

The feminine sex is not debarred from the priesthood,[30] but only a widow advanced in years is ever chosen, and that rather rarely. Unless they are women, the priests have for their wives the very finest women of the country.

To no other office in Utopia is more honor given, so much so that, even if they have committed any crime, they are subjected to no tribunal, but left only to God and to themselves. They judge it wrong to lay human hands upon one, however guilty, who has been consecrated to God in a singular manner as a holy offering. It is easier for them to observe this custom because their priests are very few and very carefully chosen.

Besides, it does not easily happen that one who is ele-

30. Women performed sacerdotal functions in Greek and Roman religions, as well as in some early Christian sects (Aug. *De haer.* 27).

vated to such dignity for being the very best among the good, nothing but virtue being taken into account, should fall into corruption and wickedness. Even if it does happen, human nature being ever prone to change, yet since they are but few and are invested with no power except the influence of honor, it need not be feared that they will cause any great harm to the state. In fact, the reason for having but few and exceptional priests is to prevent the dignity of the order, which they now reverence very highly, from being cheapened by communicating the honor to many. This is especially true since they think it hard to find many men so good as to be fit for so honorable a position for the filling of which it is not enough to be endowed with ordinary virtues.

They are not more esteemed among their own people than among foreign nations. This can easily be seen from a fact which, I think, is its cause. When the armies are fighting in battle, the priests are to be found separate but not very far off, settled on their knees, dressed in their sacred vestments. With hands outstretched to heaven,[31] they pray first of all for peace, next for a victory to their own side—but without much bloodshed on either side. When their side is winning, they run among the combatants and restrain the fury of their own men against the routed enemy. Merely to see and to appeal to them suffices to save one's life; to touch their flowing garments protects one's remaining goods from every harm arising from war.

This conduct has brought them such veneration among all nations everywhere and has given them so real a majesty that they have saved their own citizens from the enemy as often as they have protected the enemy from their own men. The following is well known. Sometimes their own side had given way, their case had been des-

31. Like those of Moses against the Amalekites (Exod. 17:12).

perate, they were taking to flight, and the enemy was rushing on to kill and to plunder. Then the carnage had been averted by the intervention of the priests. After the armies had been parted from each other, peace had been concluded and settled on just terms. Never had there been any nation so savage, cruel, and barbarous that it had not regarded their persons as sacred and inviolable.

They celebrate as holydays the first and the last day of each month and likewise of each year. The latter they divide into months, measured by the orbit of the moon just as the course of the sun rounds out the year. In their language they call the first days Cynemerni and the last days Trapemerni.[32] These names have the same meaning as if they were rendered "First-Feasts" and "Final-Feasts."

Their temples are fine sights, not only elaborate in workmanship but also capable of holding a vast throng, and necessarily so, since there are so few of them. The temples are all rather dark. This feature, they report, is due not to an ignorance of architecture but to the deliberate intention of the priests. They think that excessive light makes the thoughts wander, whereas scantier and uncertain light concentrates the mind and conduces to devotion.

In Utopia, as has been seen, the religion of all is not the same, and yet all its manifestations, though varied and manifold, by different roads as it were, tend to the same end, the worship of the divine nature. Therefore nothing is seen or heard in the temples which does not seem to agree with all in common. If any sect has a rite of its own, it is performed within the walls of each man's home. Public worship is conducted according to a ritual which does not at all detract from any of the private devotions. Therefore no image of the gods is seen in the temple so that the individual may be free to conceive

32. *Cynemerni* 'Dog-Days,' or 'Starting-Days,' or 'Rogation-Days.' *Trapemerni* 'Turning-Days' or 'Closing-Days' (ibid.).

of God with the most ardent devotion in any form he
pleases. They invoke God by no special name except
that of Mithras. By this word they agree to represent the
one nature of the divine majesty whatever it be. The
prayers formulated are such as every man may utter without offense to his own belief.

On the evening of the Final-Feasts, they gather in the
temple, still fasting. They thank God for the prosperity
they have enjoyed in the month or year of which that
holyday is the last day. Next day, which is the First-
Feast, they flock to the temples in the morning. They
pray for good luck and prosperity in the ensuing year
or month, of which this holyday is the auspicious beginning.

On the Final-Feasts, before they go to the temple,
wives fall down at the feet of their husbands, children
at the feet of their parents. They confess that they have
erred, either by committing some fault or by performing
some duty carelessly, and beg pardon for their offense.
Hence, if any cloud of quarrel in the family has arisen,
it is dispelled by this satisfaction so that with pure and
clear minds they may be present at the sacrifices, for they
are too scrupulous to attend with a troubled conscience.
If they are aware of hatred or anger against anyone they
do not assist at the sacrifices until they have been recon-
ciled and have cleansed their hearts, for fear of swift
and great punishment.

When they reach the temple, they part, the men going
to the right side and the women to the left. Then they
arrange their places so that the males in each home sit
in front of the head of the household and the women-
folk are in front of the mother of the family. They thus
take care that every gesture of everyone abroad is observed by those whose authority and discipline govern
them at home. They also carefully see to it that everywhere the younger are placed in the company of the

elder. If children were trusted to children, they might spend in childish foolery the time in which they ought to be conceiving a religious fear toward the gods, the greatest and almost the only stimulus to the practice of virtues.

They slay no animal in their sacrifices. They do not believe that the divine clemency delights in bloodshed and slaughter, seeing that it has imparted life to animate creatures that they might enjoy life. They burn incense and other' fragrant substances and also offer a great number of candles. They are not unaware that these things add nothing to the divine nature, any more than do human prayers, but they like this harmless kind of worship. Men feel that, by these sweet smells and lights, as well as the other ceremonies, they somehow are uplifted and rise with livelier devotion to the worship of God.

The people are clothed in white garments in the temple. The priest wears vestments of various colors, of wonderful design and shape, but not of material as costly as one would expect. They are not interwoven with gold or set with precious stones but wrought with the different feathers of birds[33] so cleverly and artistically that no costly material could equal the value of the handiwork. Moreover, in these birds' feathers and plumes and the definite order and plan by which they are set off on the priest's vestment, they say certain hidden mysteries are contained. By knowing the meaning as it is carefully handed down by the priests, they are reminded of God's benefits toward them and, in turn, of their own piety toward God and their duty toward one another.

As soon as the priest thus arrayed appears from the vestibule, all immediately fall on the ground in reverence. The silence all around is so deep that the very

33. A detail perhaps suggested by the American Indians.

appearance of the congregation strikes one with awe as
if some divine power were really present. After remaining a while on the ground, at a signal from the priest
they rise.

At this point they sing praises to God, which they
diversify with musical instruments, largely different in
shape from those seen in our part of the world. Very
many of them surpass in sweetness those in use with us,
but some are not even comparable with ours. But in
one respect undoubtedly they are far ahead of us. All
their music, whether played on instruments or sung by
the human voice, so renders and expresses the natural
feelings, so suits the sound to the matter (whether the
words be supplicatory, or joyful, or propitiatory, or
troubled, or mournful, or angry), and so represents the
meaning by the form of the melody that it wonderfully
affects, penetrates, and inflames the souls of the hearers.[34]

At the end, the priest and the people together repeat
solemn prayers fixed in form, so drawn up that each
individual may apply to himself personally what all
recite together. In these prayers every man recognizes
God to be the author of creation and governance and
all other blessings besides. He thanks Him for all the
benefits received, particularly that by the divine favor
he has chanced on that commonwealth which is the happiest and has received that religion which he hopes to
be the truest. If he errs in these matters or if there is
anything better and more approved by God than that
commonwealth or that religion, he prays that He will,
of His goodness, bring him to the knowledge of it, for
he is ready to follow in whatever path He may lead him.[35]
But if this form of a commonwealth be the best and his

34. "The music and the rhythm must follow the speech" (Pl. *Rep.*
3.398D). Erasmus and others advocated plain chant.

35. More advises men "to pray unto God . . . that it might please
Him to help them in the way of the right belief" (*Works,* p. 581).

religion the truest, he prays that then He may give him steadfastness and bring all other mortals to the same way of living and the same opinion of God—unless there be something in this variety of religions which delights His inscrutable will.

Finally, he prays that God will take him to Himself by an easy death, how soon or late he does not venture to determine. However, if it might be without offense to His Majesty, it would be much more welcome to him to die a very hard death and go to God than to be kept longer away from Him even by a very prosperous career in life.[36]

After this prayer has been said, they prostrate themselves on the ground again. Then shortly they rise and go away to dinner. The rest of the day they pass in games and in exercises of military training.

Now I have described to you, as exactly as I could, the structure of that commonwealth which I judge not merely the best but the only one which can rightly claim the name of a commonwealth. Outside Utopia, to be sure, men talk freely of the public welfare—but look after their private interests only. In Utopia, where nothing is private, they seriously concern themselves with public affairs. Assuredly in both cases they act reasonably. For, outside Utopia, how many are there who do not realize that, unless they make some separate provision for themselves, however flourishing the commonwealth, they will themselves starve? For this reason, necessity compels them to hold that they must take account of themselves rather than of the people, that is, of others.

On the other hand, in Utopia, where everything belongs to everybody, no one doubts, provided only that

36. In prison More wrote: "I never have prayed God to bring me hence nor deliver me from death" (*S.L.*, p. 238).

the public granaries are well filled, that the individual will lack nothing for his private use. The reason is that the distribution of goods is not niggardly. In Utopia there is no poor man and no beggar. Though no man has anything, yet all are rich.

For what can be greater riches for a man than to live with a joyful and peaceful mind, free of all worries— not troubled about his food or harassed by the querulous demands of his wife or fearing poverty for his son or worrying about his daughter's dowry, but feeling secure about the livelihood and happiness of himself and his family: wife, sons, grandsons, great-grandsons, great-great-grandsons, and all the long line of their descendants that gentlefolk anticipate? Then take into account the fact that there is no less provision for those who are now helpless but once worked than for those who are still working.

At this point I should like anyone to be so bold as to compare this fairness with the so-called justice prevalent in other nations, among which, upon my soul, I cannot discover the slightest trace of justice and fairness. What brand of justice is it that any nobleman whatsoever or goldsmith-banker or moneylender or, in fact, anyone else from among those who either do no work at all or whose work is of a kind not very essential to the commonwealth, should attain a life of luxury and grandeur on the basis of his idleness or his nonessential work? In the meantime, the common laborer, the carter, the carpenter, and the farmer perform work so hard and continuous that beasts of burden could scarcely endure it and work so essential that no commonwealth could last even one year without it. Yet they earn such scanty fare and lead such a miserable life that the condition of beasts of burden might seem far preferable. The latter do not have to work so incessantly nor is their food much worse (in fact, sweeter to their taste) nor do they entertain any fear for the future. The workmen, on the other hand, not only have to toil and suffer without return or profit in the present but agonize over the thought of an indigent old age. Their daily wage is too scanty to suffice even for the day: much less is there an excess and surplus that daily can be laid by for their needs in old age.

Now is not this an unjust and ungrateful commonwealth? It lavishes great rewards on so-called gentlefolk and banking goldsmiths and the rest of that kind, who are either idle or mere parasites and purveyors of empty pleasures. On the contrary, it makes no benevolent provision for farmers, colliers, common laborers, carters, and carpenters without whom there would be no commonwealth at all. After it has misused the labor of their prime and after they are weighed down with age and disease and are in utter want, it forgets all their sleepless nights and all the great benefits received at their hands and most ungratefully requites them with a most miserable death.

What is worse, the rich every day extort a part of their daily allowance from the poor not only by private fraud but by public law. Even before they did so it seemed unjust that persons deserving best of the commonwealth should have the worst return. Now they have further distorted and debased the right and, finally, by making laws, have palmed it off as justice. Consequently, when I consider and turn over in my mind the state of all commonwealths flourishing anywhere today, so help me God, I can see nothing else than a kind of conspiracy of the rich, who are aiming at their own interests under the name and title of the commonwealth. They invent and devise all ways and means by which, first, they may keep without fear of loss all that they have amassed by evil practices and, secondly, they may then purchase as cheaply as possible and abuse the toil and labor of all the poor. These devices become law as soon as the rich have once decreed their observance in the name of the public—that is, of the poor also![37]

Yet when these evil men with insatiable greed have divided up among themselves all the goods which would have been enough for all the people, how far they are from the happiness of the Utopian commonwealth! In Utopia all greed for money was entirely removed with the use of money. What a mass of troubles was then cut away! What a crop of crimes was then pulled up by the roots! Who does not know that fraud, theft, rapine, quarrels, disorders, brawls, seditions, murders, treasons, poisonings, which are avenged rather than restrained by daily executions, die out with the destruction of money? Who does not know that fear, anxiety, worries, toils, and sleepless nights will also perish at the same time as money? What is more, poverty, which alone money seemed to make poor, forthwith would itself dwindle and disappear if money were entirely done away with everywhere.[38]

To make this assertion clearer, consider in your thoughts some barren and unfruitful year in which many thousands of men have been carried off by famine. I emphatically contend that at the end of that scarcity, if rich men's granaries had been searched, as much grain could have been found as, if it had been divided among the people killed off by starvation and disease, would have prevented anyone from feeling that meager return from soil and climate. So easily might men get the necessities of life if that blessed money, supposedly a grand

37. "The oligarchical statesmen ought to pretend to be speaking on behalf of the people" (Arist. *Pol.* 5.7.19, 1310a).

38. Sallust tells Caesar that the whole world will be "set in order by land and sea . . . if you deprive money, which is the root of all evil, of its advantage and honor" (*Ad Caes. Or.* 7.1–3).

invention to ease access to those necessities, was not in fact the only barrier to our getting what we need.[39]

Even the rich, I doubt not, have such feelings. They are not unaware that it would be a much better state of affairs to lack no necessity than to have abundance of superfluities—to be snatched from such numerous troubles rather than to be hemmed in by great riches. Nor does it occur to me to doubt that a man's regard for his own interests or the authority of Christ our Savior—who in His wisdom could not fail to know what was best and who in His goodness would not fail to counsel what He knew to be best—would long ago have brought the whole world to adopt the laws of the Utopian commonwealth, had not one single monster, the chief and progenitor of all plagues, striven against it—I mean, Pride.[40]

Pride measures prosperity not by her own advantages but by others' disadvantages. Pride would not consent to be made even a goddess if no poor wretches were left for her to domineer over and scoff at, if her good fortune might not dazzle by comparison with their miseries, if the display of her riches did not torment and intensify their poverty. This serpent from hell entwines itself around the hearts of men and acts like the suckfish in preventing and hindering them from entering on a better way of life.[41]

Pride is too deeply fixed in men to be easily plucked out. For this reason, the fact that this form of a commonwealth—which I should gladly desire for all—has been

39. The "natural necessaries are not in every case readily portable; hence . . . men made a mutual compact to give and accept some substance . . . easy to handle in use for general life" (Arist. *Pol.* 1.3.13–14, 1257a).

40. More sees Pride as "the mischievous mother of all manner vice" (*Works*, p. 82).

41. Although small, the suckfish (Lat. *remora*, Gr. *echeneis*, confused with *echinus*, 'sea urchin') was believed to have the power of attaching itself to and stopping ships (cf. Plin. *HN* 9.41, 32.1).

Book II

the good fortune of the Utopians at least, fills me with joy. They have adopted such institutions of life as have laid the foundations of the commonwealth not only most happily, but also to last forever, as far as human prescience can forecast. At home they have extirpated the roots of ambition and factionalism, along with all the other vices. Hence there is no danger of trouble from domestic discord, which has been the only cause of ruin to the well-established prosperity of many cities. As long as harmony is preserved at home and its institutions are in a healthy state, not all the envy of neighboring rulers, though it has rather often attempted it and has always been repelled, can avail to shatter or to shake that nation.

When Raphael had finished his story, many things came to my mind which seemed very absurdly established in the customs and laws of the people described—not only in their method of waging war, their ceremonies and religion, as well as their other institutions, but most of all in that feature which is the principal foundation of their whole structure. I mean their common life and subsistence—without any exchange of money. This latter alone utterly overthrows all the nobility, magnificence, splendor, and majesty which are, in the estimation of the common people, the true glories and ornaments of the commonwealth.[42]

I knew, however, that he was wearied with his tale, and I was not quite certain that he could brook any opposition to his views, particularly when I recalled his censure of others on account of their fear that they might not appear to be wise enough, unless they found some fault to criticize in other men's discoveries. I therefore praised their way of life and his speech and, taking

42. Erasmus had written More: "you are accustomed to dissent sharply from the crowd" (*Folly*, p. 2). "Nobility means ancient wealth and virtue" (Arist. *Pol.* 4.6.5, 1294a); magnificence "consists in suitable expenditure on a great scale" (*Eth. Nic.* 4.2.1, 1122a).

him by the hand, led him in to supper. I first said, nevertheless, that there would be another chance to think about these matters more deeply and to talk them over with him more fully. If only this were some day possible!

Meanwhile, though in other respects he is a man of the most undoubted learning as well as of the greatest knowledge of human affairs, I cannot agree with all that he said. But I readily admit that there are very many features in the Utopian commonwealth which it is easier for me to wish for in our countries than to have any hope of seeing realized.

END OF BOOK TWO

THE END OF THE AFTERNOON DISCOURSE OF
RAPHAEL HYTHLODAEUS ON THE LAWS
AND CUSTOMS OF THE ISLAND OF
UTOPIA, HITHERTO KNOWN BUT
TO FEW, AS REPORTED BY THE
MOST DISTINGUISHED AND
MOST LEARNED MAN,
MR. THOMAS MORE,
CITIZEN AND SHERIFF OF LONDON

FINIS

INDEX

Abraxa, 60
Achorians, the, 42
Adam of St. Victor, 37
Ademus, 73
Aegidius Romanus, xxxii, 39, 54
Aesop, 11
Africa, 107
Agincourt, battle of (1415), 23
Agnadello, battle of (1509), 40
Agricola, 11
Alaopolitans, the, ix, 119
Albany, Duke of, John Stewart, 41
Albret, John d', King of Navarre, 41
Aldus Manutius. *See* Manutius, Aldus
Alexander VI, Pope, xix, 116
Amalekites, the, 141
Amaurotum, ix, 5, 61, 63–66, 83, 86
America, 107
Ames, Russell, xxvi, xxxii
Anaxagoras of Clazomenae, 13
Anemolian ambassadors, the, xix, 86–88
Antwerp, xi, 3, 11
Anydrus River, 5, 64–65
Apina, 105
Apinatus, Tricius, 105
Apulia, 105
Ariosto, Lodovico, xii
Aristophanes, 105

Aristotle, xii, 39, 45–47, 51–52, 54, 60–61, 64, 104, 107, 149–51
Arthur, Prince, xviii
Athenaeus, 47
Athenian Academy, 115
Athos, 60
Augustinians, order of, 36

Babylon, 65
Bacon, Francis, xxxii, 43, 45, 48
Barclay, Alexander, 111
Barzanes, 73
Basel, xvi
Basilides the Gnostic, 60
Bath and Wells, Bishop of. *See* Knight, William
Benedictines, order of, 36
Beneventum, 47
Beresford, Maurice, 24, 27
Blackwell, Sir Basil, xxiv
Born, L. K., xii
Boulogne, battle of (1492), 21
Brabant, 40
Brant, Sebastian, 111
Brixius, Germanus, xxiii
Brodie, D. M., 90
Browning, Robert, xviii
Bruges, 10
Brussels, 10
Buckinghamshire, 24
Budé, William, xvi, 39
Burgomaster of Bruges. *See* Halewyn, J. de
Burgundy, Duchy of, 40

Index

Index

Index

Index

Index